My Life Acting,
Writing, and
Sometimes
Boxing

Other books by Fred Burstein

Gracie's Birds

Animal Dreams

The Way to Cattail Pond

If it Snowed Forever

The Dancer

Whispering in the Park

Anna's Rain

Rebecca's Nap

My Life Acting, Writing, and Sometimes Boxing

Fred Burstein

IRIE BOOKS

Please direct all enquiries
and wholesale orders
to Irie Books at:
gerald@geraldhausman.com

Cover and book design by
NRK Designs, Bokeelia FL 33922
nrkdesigns@gmail.com

ISBN: 978-1-5154-4820-4
First Edition
10 9 8 7 6 5 4 3 2 1

For Joe Hardy;

and the man who said,
"Why don't you write about acting?";

and always,
Fran, Rebecca, and Anna

1
Leonard

When I met Leonard in Los Angeles, in the late 70's, my life changed. He liked to think he was gruff. A gravelly voiced older man, though younger than I am now. He had been the head writer for a TV show that had been on TV for years – "The Untouchables." Big hit. But when we met he complained that the people he had to pitch his TV scripts to now weren't even born when "The Untouchables" was at the top of the charts. Somehow, now, they, "these kids," as he called them, were running his life. And ruining it too. He hadn't sold a script in years. We met at the Beverly Hills house of one of his friends, James Sheldon, the director of one of the best Twilight Zones, "It's a Good Life," about a young boy who terrorized his family with his power to turn people into scarecrows or jack-in-the-boxes. If you were at James' (never Jim, I found out the hard way) house and had somehow missed the episode he directed, you could watch it in his TV room where it played all day every day. I probably met James because of someone I met at the gym, who knew him, and got me an invitation to a party at his house.

1

Hopeful actors were happy to go to parties where well-known writers and producers and famous actors and directors met to swim and eat and god only knows what else. When I got to the director's house, I drove up the long driveway full of trees with tiny lights strung all over them, parked my sad old car beside someone's new Mercedes, walked to the front door and knocked. The cook or the housekeeper opened the door for me. I took a few steps inside the house and met Leonard. He came over to me and put his hand out. I reached over and we shook.

"You've just met the most dangerous man at this party," he said. His voice gravelly and low, like he was a gun toting killer in a B movie Western.

"Have mercy," I said. He laughed a low, gravelly laugh, one chuckle at a time, and his eyes seemed to sparkle. We were friends ever after.

Leonard saw to it that I joined a good acting class and watched lots of 'classic' movies and went to the gym every day. I met people with him that I never would have met alone. One day I found myself on the set of a Muppet movie and I met Jim Henson and watched Mel Brooks do a scene in ten different ways.

Years later, when Leonard was suicidal because no one was buying his scripts (still) and because his diabetes, which he had kept a secret, was destroying his body, he decided to move back to New York City for one last try at getting a job and staying alive. His trip back to New York did change his life, and mine too. But more about that later.

While we were still in Los Angeles, at Leonard's apartment, just off Sunset Blvd, when he was about 58 and I was about 28, and we had known each other for about a year, we were talking about actors and age and he said, "It doesn't matter how old you are. I was at a party a few years ago. All of a sudden Cary Grant walked in. He was 70 something. Everything stopped. Everybody froze. The whole room lit up!" Leonard paused dramatically for a few seconds. He made a tiny laugh in his throat that meant he had just thought of something. "When you walk into a room," he said, "it gets darker."

We didn't always get along. Sometimes, at his apartment, after I had been to an acting class during the afternoon or when my day job was done, before we would go to the Joe Allen restaurant for supper and get a Bourbon for me and a Scotch for him, he would say something to me like, "Act."

I'd say, "What do you mean, 'Act.' Here? In your apartment? Now? People don't suddenly just – 'act'."

"Sure, they do. Improvise," he'd say.

"You know," I'd say, "you might be a good writer, and you might be a pretty good manager, but you suck as an acting coach. I'm hungry. Let's go eat."

But he wouldn't give in. My anger would grow until I either left or maybe did a stupid little acting scene. One night, I got so mad I picked up his coffee table and threw it across the living room, then I left and drove back in my old crappy car to my own little place a couple of miles down the road between Sunset Blvd. and Hollywood Blvd. The rent there was cheaper, and the street corners were crowded with prostitutes. They looked so tough I never went near them. After I threw the coffee table we didn't talk or meet for weeks. I thought — fine, who needs him. I can get acting work without him. How much has he really done for me?

While I was having a coffee-and-bagel break at the travel agency I worked at, a call came in. Calls came in all the time. My job didn't include answering the phone. The woman who did answer said, "Certainly sir, one moment sir," and then she sang out, "Frehh-dee, it's for you-oo!"

I picked up my phone. "Hello?"

Leonard waited a second and then said in his deepest gravel voice, "So what are you doing these days besides looking at your ass in the mirror?" I laughed pretty hard. How could I stay mad? That night we had dinner and drinks and talked about acting again at "Joe Allen."

1.5
Grease

My acting class met during the day
in a small room in a quiet part of LA.
The more experienced actors met at night
— with the better teacher.
We day-timers acted short scenes and our teacher,
not much more experienced than we were,
would tell us what to change or do over
or not do any more.
As if he knew.
There was one student, a little older than I was,
who I thought was wasting his time.
He'd never get a job, I thought.
He came in one day and told us all
that he just got a job.
"It's a movie," he said.
"Something called 'Grease.'
I think John Travolta
from *Welcome Back, Kotter* is in it.
Ever hear of him?"

"Yeah, I've seen that show," I said.
"Congratulations! What's your part like?" I asked.
"I'm going to be a race car driver.
I think Travolta and I race each other."
His name was Dennis Stewart.
And he did race John Travolta
In something called *Grease*.

2
Missing Maine

Yes, I'd get really mad and say that Leonard never really did anything good for me, so why should I care if we never saw each other again. But of course that wasn't true. He did a lot. I met actors and producers and directors with him. I studied acting with Stella Adler for a year and went with him to Lee Strasberg's home, where I walked around and looked at the books on his bookshelf, being too bashful or too theatrically uneducated to talk to him or any of the other guests. Maybe he'll think I'm the strong silent type, I thought, maybe he'll do all he can to get me a good part in a great movie. Or even a great part in a good movie. Never saw Lee again.

I joined a group of actors and writers who met every week to work on plays and give each other writing and acting critiques. Leonard was one of the writers. A couple of other actors and I presented scenes from a play Leonard was

7

working on and directing. (No one liked the play much.) Carroll O'Connor came in one night. He was ready to watch scenes, but no one had anything ready to act out. Everyone scrambled to come up with something to show the big star, to no avail.

Leonard made sure I got my SAG card, which is a big deal. It wasn't easy to get into the Screen Actors Guild in those days. It probably still isn't. You couldn't act in a Union TV show or movie, (most shows) unless you had a Screen Actor's card, and you couldn't get the card unless someone hired you to be in a Union show. The exception was, as I understood it, if the casting people couldn't find a Union actor with the right eye color or the right space between his front teeth or the right size of biceps, they could hire a non-union person who did have what they needed. Which kind of threw it wide open. Then the actor had to join the Union to be in the show. Which is what the actor wanted to do all along. I think I had just the right perfectly straight ancient Greek nose. (This was before I was splitting firewood years later by banging a wedge into the wood with a sledgehammer and the wedge shot out of the wood at a hundred miles an hour and flew into my nose, making it forever rough and tough. I tell people, "Ha! You should see the log!") So, Leonard's friend, the one who had the parties and the pool and the TV that played the "Twilight Zone" episode he directed on a 24 hour loop, told the casting directors that he wanted me in his next show because he needed my straight nose for a close-up. So, not only did I meet Ken Curtis, who played Festus on "Gunsmoke," but I got my Screen Actors' Guild card, which I still have, all these decades later. But before there was Leonard and unions and auditions, there was the task of getting me out of rural Maine and into Los Angeles. My older brother took that job.

Darrell is three years older than I am. I shared a bedroom with him in our little house from soon after I was born until he went to college 15 years later. Once I was out of the crib, I slept in a bed that was next to his with a night table between us. Sharing a room with him was often diffi-cult. When we were older, he always went to bed about the time I had already fallen asleep. He opened our bedroom door and came into our room and left the door open while he went down the hall to brush his teeth in the bathroom. The hall light beamed into the bedroom and smacked me awake. When he came back to our room, he took his shoes off and it sounded like he dropped them from over his head to the floor, next to my bed, so if I *had* begun to fall asleep again, I woke up immediately. I don't know why his shoes were raised up high before they were dropped to the floor, since they had spent the whole day on the floor to begin with, but maybe it was some kind of secret ritual. Maybe at that hour, in that room, after all those years, he just didn't acknowledge my existence. But when I got older and lived in Maine for a couple of years, and he was already a doctor in California, he more than acknowledged my existence: he saved it. "

What are you going to do now," he asked on a phone call from California to Maine in the 70's.

I was 26, my two-year marriage had just ended, the house I had bought when I got married was sold, and I wasn't employed as a school bus driver anymore. "I don't know,"

I said. "Maybe work in a mill at night here in Maine, and finish college during the day. Or buy a small place here in Maine with the money from selling the divorce house and find a job in a mill and try to write something when I'm not working. Or maybe become an actor."

"It all sounds, uh…really great," he said."

"You think so?" I asked.

"Uh, no," he said. "It sounds like a damned nightmare."

"Well, Kafka worked all day and then wrote at home in the middle of the night," I countered.

"Well, let me say this – about that. You are not Kafka. No one is, except Kafka. And God willing, you won't die of laryngeal tuberculosis when you are 41, like he did. Why don't you come to California and stay with me for a while. Los Angeles is a pretty good place to work on becoming an actor, you know. Or anything else."

I wondered if he would still wake me up every night if I moved in with him in California. "Well. What about your girlfriend?" I asked.

"No. You can't have her. But there are lots of other women out here. Maybe one of them would like you."

"I just meant…"

"I know what you meant. Come out here and let's see what happens."

I flew out not long after that and he picked me up at the LA Airport in his new red Porsche (making sure I called it a 'porsh uh' and never a 'porsh') (license plate with his initials, a space, then MD). So, he took me to the house he rented on a hill in Beverly Hills. We probably went out to eat that night, and then I went to sleep in the spare room.

In the morning I woke up listening to what I thought were trees in Maine rustling in the wind outside my window. I smiled, happy. Trees and rivers and wind blew into the room and made me happy. I could feel them. I hurried to the window to see the bright new leaves and the sun sparkling on the water.

Instead, looking down from the hill the house sat on, I saw thousands of cars on a highway, half-speeding north, the other half speeding south. There was no beginning or end to the cars and no spaces between them. A cloud of orange-brown smoke from their exhaust pipes came up to the hill I was on. Smoke that had been growing thicker and more deadly for decades

When I went downstairs to eat breakfast, Darrell had already gone to his office. He left a note that said, "Eat. Look around." His girlfriend, Dana, was already out too, looking for a house for Darrell to buy. She had a real estate license and went searching for a house every day. Darrell never liked any of them. She kept looking. Darrell was about 30 and she was about 50. I didn't think they had much of a future together if she ever did find a house he liked. (Eventually she did find a house he liked. He bought it, moved into it, bought her a Mercedes, and broke up with her. Maybe not in that order. But years later I got a call from *her* that changed my life. Again.)

After breakfast I went outside. It was warm and sunny, and flowers dangled from anything they could grab on to — drain pipes, fences, trees, mailboxes. There were flowers and vines everywhere.

The house next to Darrell's was lower on the hill. A young

woman who might have been home from college for the summer was standing in the sun on the porch, maybe picking up the morning paper or just glad to be home, surrounded by the bougainvillea that climbed and swayed all around her. She was still in her nightgown, which was made of thin red threads that didn't hide her body so much as give it a reddish tint. She didn't seem to notice me. She had no intention of saying, "Good morning." I still see her in my thoughts whenever the sun is out, flowers are blooming, and the day is beginning. She is naked but tinted red, wearing that transparent nightgown as she turns to go back inside.

A week went by, and though I had hardly gone anywhere or done anything, I decided to leave and go back to Maine and buy a place to live. I missed Maine. I had friends there. I had land there that I could put some kind of small house on. I could get a job. I told Darrell I was going to leave. I had given California and an acting career a shot, and it didn't work out. But it was nice that he let me stay with him so I could give it a chance.

"You're going to go back to... (dramatic pause here, as if the word was almost impossible to say) Maine?" he said.

"Yeah. I'm not getting anywhere here...so...I might as well go back while I still have some money left from selling the house." He looked angry. "Are you mad?"

"Mad? Why would I be mad? What do I care if you leave."

He sounded mad. I said, "I just think...I don't know. It doesn't seem like anything is going to happen and I better go back while I still have some money left and I can..."

"You want to go, just go. It doesn't matter to me. Why the hell should I care. It's your life. Go back to freezing Maine."

I didn't want it to end that way. He was in our old bedroom again, unaware of my existence, dropping his shoes to the floor. I was already invisible to him, and gone. There was nothing for him to deal with anymore. Time for bed.

I can't remember what I did the next day. I probably called some place about flights back East and started re-packing my suitcase.

I expected mostly silence from Darrell when he got home from work, and that at some point I would just have to say, "Goodbye, and thanks for everything."

But when he got home, he walked over to me and took a breath. "You can't leave," he said.

"I just ordered a…" I began.

"No. Call them back. You can't leave. You have to stay here in Los Angeles. You've got to at least meet the people I know who can help you. And you have to spend some time really working at this. You haven't done anything yet. So unpack, because you are not leaving. You can't."

Thank God Darrell insisted. LA was my home for the next 5 years, and my life became so much different.

2.5
House Hunting

It was breakfast, Sunday morning,
and Darrell was reading the news
in The LA Times
and Dana was looking at the real estate pages.
I was looking at Help Wanted ads.
Dana started laughing hysterically.
"Oh my god!" she said. "Listen to this typo!
'Large, newly renovated home with a
gorgeous view.
Pool, yard and garage.
This home also comes with a huge dick,
perfect for grilling
or just lying in the sun!"
"Sounds delightful," Darrell said.

3
Getting Started

The first thing Darrell did to start my acting career, besides keeping me in California, and maybe the most important thing he did, was to get me a membership at the Beverly Hill Health Club, or, as we called it, the gym. It wasn't really in Beverly Hills, but it was close.

One way or another, all the people I met who brought me closer to being in show business can be traced back to the gym. Not to mention that it was a fun place, with Jacuzzis that you put a quarter in to make the bubbles start, Ancient Roman style white robes given to us to walk around in after the Jacuzzi, lots of weights, and bars to do pull-ups on.

There were metal clamps that snapped on to the bottom of your legs with hooks that you could attach to the overhead pull-up bar and then hang upside-down, with your head and arms almost touching the floor, and let your back stretch and straighten and relax.

One afternoon I was hanging upside down like that with my eyes closed. I was letting my back sink down, lower, lower. I had hurt one of the disks in my spine in the gym in Maine before I went to California and hanging upside down after the hot tub seemed to be helping. I heard one of the men I knew say to a friend, "What the hell is he doing there hanging upside-down? Is he dead?"

"Dead. Or meditating," the other man said. "Can you meditate upside down? Hey, Fred. Are you alive?"

A laugh began inside my head that spread to my toes and grew stronger and stronger until I was swinging side to side laughing upside down. I managed to un-hook my feet from the bar I hung from and stand up the normal way so I could breathe better.

"Are you trying to kill me?" I asked when I calmed down.

"We were afraid you were already dead."

There was a sunbathing area outside the gym that was kept hidden from the people on Santa Monica Blvd by a wooden fence completely overgrown with red flowering bougainvillea vines. Naked men, well oiled, well tanned, rested in the sun on lounge chairs on one side of the fence and people wearing clothes were going about their business walking along the sidewalk on the other side of the fence. There was a basketball court in a corner of the gym's outdoor area, where Peter Falk played almost every day. He was a fierce player. You could hear him yelling about something all the time.

I never met Peter Falk, but I met other people at the gym who introduced me to their friends who didn't go to the gym; people who were rich enough to have their own hot tubs and weight rooms and private trainers.

It was at the gym that I met the ex-bandleader (can't remember his name) who invited me to TV director James Sheldon's house, and this was where I met Leonard.

"I had a big limousine," the band leader told me when

we were yelling over the noise of the Jacuzzi bubbles one day. "My license plate said "MUSIC." A chauffeur would drive me to my gigs, and my band and I played the biggest fucking venues. Shit! People yelled and screamed and drank and danced their fat asses off." He wiped his sweaty face and looked around at the other men in the other sections of the Jacuzzi. "Now I'm lying around here most of the day in a Roman smock, like a fucking shmuck, or boiling in this hot water."

"What happened?" I asked.

"Ha! It's what *always* happens! Every *freaking* time! To everybody! My accountant, who was also my best goddamn friend, stole every penny I had and disappeared!"

"Well, at least now you can relax and steam," I said.

"Yes, true. I can sit and shvitz all day now."

3.5
On the way to the Gym

Darrell got me a membership
to the Beverly Hills Health Club
a few weeks after I moved in with him.
As I was driving there on the Santa Monica Blvd.
I had to go through a break in the median
because the gym was on the other side
of the road.
With my signal blinking, I turned right
while a car crossing the median on the other side,
from the other direction
almost ran into me.
My window was down and so was his
And I yelled to the driver
A phrase I brought with me from Maine:
"You fucking son of a whore!"
Well, that did it!
He slammed on his breaks
And all 4 doors of his car opened
And four men jumped out.

I was in a fearless, suicidal mood
so I stopped *my* car
and jumped out too.
When the driver reached under his seat
And pulled out a long steel crowbar,
My fighting spirit left me.
"Hold it!" I said, "Get rid of the crowbar!"
"Fuck you!" he said.
"You called my mother a whore!"
I wanted to tell him it was nothing personal.
That's just how we talk
where I lived in Maine.
He and the other men kept walking toward me.
He held up the crowbar. "This is my *equalizer*,"
he said.
He added, "Look how fucking *big* you are!"
I almost said, "Wait…you think I'm *big*? Really!"
I felt like asking them all into the gym for
lunch. On me.
But I just said, "Nah, I'm not fighting a man
with a crowbar and 3 other men too.
I'm done."
Somehow that worked.

I got back into my car
and they got back into their car.
I drove into the gym lot, parked, and went in.
I showed the man at the door my
membership card,
Went to the cafeteria,
and ordered some of their fantastic,
corned beef.

Story 4
Rock Hard

I had an old car I bought in LA with some of my divorce money and I had a gym membership that Darrell bought me, so now it was time to get a job on a TV show or in a movie. I still lived with Darrell and his girlfriend. Darrell pointed out to me, after a month, that it was probably time to get my own place. And it was. Before I left Darrell's house for good I walked over to a small and expensive meat market that was in the San Fernando Valley, down the hill from Darrell's place, and bought a piece of pork, some kind of loin roast, to make for him and his girlfriend as a "thank you." The meat was very expensive, so I thought it would automatically taste good.

There was no internet in those days so I looked in a cook book I found in the house that had a recipe for the pork. I cooked it in Darrell's oven for supper that night and it came out something like a sheepskin rug that had been thrown out of a wagon crossing Death Valley on the way to the coast about a hundred and fifty years ago. Any taste, except for tongue burning salt, had evaporated completely before it left the oven. Chewing the pork was difficult. Swallowing it was out of the question.

"Thanks Fred. This was nice of you," Darrell said while pretending to wipe his face so he could sneak the chunk of meat he had been gnawing into the napkin.

"It's a little tough, I guess," I said. "I hope it's alright."

"Well, yeah, it is a *little* tough, but that's okay. Where did you get it?"

"I went to that place down the hill that you told me you go to."

"Oh yeah. He's got the best meat. Funny guy, huh. Likes to talk a lot."

"Yeah. Sure does. He told me all about how long he ages his meat," I said while I chewed. "I thought I was going to be there while it aged a few more months. Loves to talk!"

"Yeah. Expensive, but good," Darrell said.

At least none of us died that night.

I moved out of Darrell's house to a little place on a dead-end dirt road behind the hill that the HOLLYWOOD sign sits on. When you looked down from my new apartment you could see the sign, but because you were behind it, the letters were all backwards.

My cousin Lois lived in the upstairs apartment with her boyfriend, and I moved into the one-room apartment near ground level. The walls of the house were made of cinder-blocks. Darrell bought me a double bed for the place. "In case you get lucky," he said.

Now I had a place to live, but I needed a job. And once

again help came from the gym. Someone at the gym told me he had a friend who was an accountant who was looking for a bookkeeper to work at a travel agency. The only books I had ever kept were the kind with stories in them, but I went to see the man anyway. I told him I had no experience, wasn't great at math, and didn't know what a bookkeeper did. He said, "Okay, you're hired."

The office was in one of the two triangular skyscrapers in Century City. Fancy. The owner of the agency, a man, and one of its agents, a woman, were from Sweden. They were both in their late 50's. The owner was gruff and curt. One of the rare men I've met here, I thought, who was straight. Until one day we took the elevator to look at another office higher up in the building that he was thinking of renting. He squeezed a big lump that had grown inside his pants and said, "You make me hard as a fucking rock."

"Really? I'm, well, um…that's nice," I said, "but… I'm not…"

"Well," he said, squeezing the lump harder, "I guess I'll have to go home then and bang this thing on the windowsill a few hundred times."

I couldn't see how that would help, but I was glad he didn't press the issue. Later that day I said to a friend at the office, who I knew was gay, "I had no idea Carl was gay."

"Gay?" the man said. "Gay!? Oh, my <u>Gowd</u>, he's gayer than a box full of blue-eyed owls."

4.5
My Bike

After I lived in LA for a while,
I started riding my bike everywhere.
I liked riding it.
Just before I had left Maine,
I bought a used Honda 500 motorcycle.
I wasn't working anymore.
I'm not sure I knew what I was going to do next.
The motorcycle was fun, once I learned
how to ride it,
but I didn't want one in LA.
In Maine, I rode my motorcycle at 70 mph
with both hands up in the air
on the long empty roads.
But I couldn't do that in LA.
So I got a bike.
I rode the bike down-hill sometimes
with both hands up in the air
and once I was flying down-hill

and I went right into a hole in the road
and flew right off the bike.
When I landed, I was sitting on the bike again.
Thank God we were going the same speed!
One night I was riding up Wilshire Boulevard.
The traffic light ahead was red but I knew
that it would be green when I got to it,
so I rode full speed along-side the traffic
that had stopped
and flew out, as the light turned green,
into the intersection.
I didn't know that as I sped
to the North under the new green light,
a truck was going full speed to the East
because his light had just turned red.
I saw the truck speeding toward me
and I knew he would hit me.
I knew I would die.
It was inevitable. I was calm.
I didn't feel being hit
and then flying to the other side
of the intersection.

I didn't know the bike got hit and twisted in half.
I just remember people coming to me to help.
I remember later on I was told the driver
was handcuffed
because there was a prior warrant out
for his arrest.
And I remember before they put me
in the ambulance
and took me to the hospital,
The truck driver looked down at me
lying on the road
and said, "I'm sorry."

Story 5
Nude Beach

I became friends with a bunch of people at the gym who weren't actors. One of those friends was Miguel. We met soon after I joined the gym. I hadn't known him for very long. It seemed he just disappeared one day, but we did some things together that I'm happy to remember.

The only thing I didn't like about him was that he thought Darrell was just the cutest thing. The first time Miguel saw Darrell at the gym he said, "Who *zat*!" I said, "Oh, that's my brother." Miguel said, "No <u>way</u>! He's so good *lookin'*. How *could* he be your brother!" The first thing Miguel used to say to me when I got to the gym was, "Hi Swee' harr! Howzuh good lookin' one?" I liked to think that he was just trying to make me mad, but I think he kind of meant it.

Miguel asked me if I had ever been to the nude beach, a few miles north of Santa Monica beach. I told him I hadn't, so we decided to go. Two important things happened the day we went, which seems about a thousand years ago now. One of the things I still treasure and the other taught me an invaluable lesson. The lesson story is fast and easy. If you are at the nude beach for the first time and you are white and naked put sunscreen on your dick. If you don't you will end up with a dick that looks like a red chili pepper and burns like one for days. If you are black, I would still use the sunscreen.

Miguel picked me up and we headed West, to have lunch on the Santa Monica Beach boardwalk before we headed north to the nude beach.

The boardwalk went from the beach straight out into the ocean. There were all kinds of stores and places to eat and places to fish. Hundreds of people walked around and sped by on skateboards and roller skates and leaned out over the wooden rails to watch the ocean and talk. Miguel and I stopped at a little place along the boardwalk that made hamburgers and hotdogs and had cold drinks. There were paintings on the back wall of the place, above the stoves, of all sorts of things. The paintings looked old. Maybe the man who ran the place painted them or maybe someone painted them a long time ago. The paintings were of trees and animals and rivers. There were goats and whales and near one of the river paintings was a painting of a mud skipper.

That surprised me. They weren't on display very often. In fact, this was the first time I had ever seen a picture or painting of one since I had my own live mud skipper years earlier when I worked at a housing project in Connecticut. I had a dog back then, so I went to the pet shop for food and brushes and other dog things. I walked around to see the other animals whenever I was there. I loved pet shops.

When I was a kid I wanted to grow up and work in a pet shop. I used to practice shredding newspapers by hand so I could show the pet shop owner, when I applied for a job, that I was good at shredding. I figured that was important because shredded newspapers were used on the floors in all the cages back then for the animals' bedding. I learned that if I held the newspaper one way, the shreds would come out lop-sided and uneven and were no good really, but if I turned the paper sideways and tore it, the shreds were all straight and even and nice and thin. Perfect to fluff-up and spread on the cage floors. I was sure that when I got older and looked for a job at a pet shop my shredding talents would make me a shoe-in. So, when I went for dog food one day there was a fish tank that had shallow water in it and some stones that rose up out of the water and there were the strangest little animals sitting on the stones and a few bathing in the water.

"What are those?" I asked the pet shop man.

"Ah, those my friend are Mudskippers. From Africa! They're fish but they go on muddy land to catch bugs an' stuff to eat. They climb trees and jump, or skip around. In the mud."

I bought one on the spot. He told me what to feed it and how to set up a tank for it and I took it home.

While we were waiting for the food to cook on the grill, I told Miguel about my mud skipper. "See that funny looking thing near the bottom," I asked him as I pointed to the painted mud skipper on the back wall.

"That little brown thing, Swee' har?" he asked.

"Yes, that brown fish with the fat head. That's a mud skipper," I told him.

"That thing is a fish!" he said.

"Yep. A very special kind of fish. They live in Africa and other countries, and they live in water but they come out and walk around in the mud and catch bugs to eat. They hop and jump all around. That's why they call them 'mud skippers.' They skip from place to place and eat bugs. They can stay out of the water for a couple of days and then they must go back in the water and breathe some more. I had one once."

"Sweet har, *you* had a mud skipper? Oh my gohhd! When?"

"A few years ago. When I worked at a housing project in Connecticut. I mowed the lawns and unclogged sinks and toilets. I even shingled roofs. I had my own apartment there and I had a dog and when I went to buy some dog food I saw the mudskippers at the pet shop – and I got one." We both stood watching the man behind the counter cook our hamburgers and take new orders. The smoke was delicious.

"Did you bring him to California?" Miguel asked.

"Well, what happened was I kept it at my apartment for a while and then I brought it to the maintenance office so I could see him during the day. And the other guys liked him too. One day I hung the weed whacker when I was done on the wall sideways above the mud skipper tank and when I came back later that afternoon the mud skipper was dead."

"Swee' har'! What happened? The poor mud *skipper*!"

"It was so stupid. I was stupid. Oil leaked out of the weed whacker that I put on the wall, and it killed my mud skipper."

"Oh – that's so sad! I have a friend who has a pet shop and I'm going to tell him to get me a mud skipper. I'm going to give it to you, Sweet' har'."

Before I could answer him, the cook put two paper plates with hamburgers and hot oily French fries on the shelf in front of us.

"Let me pay," I said to Miguel. "You drove."

I reached into my back pocket and took out my wallet. "How much?" I asked.

The cook smiled. "Nothing," he said. "I liked your story. It was worth two hamburgers, easy. Enjoy."

"Really? You mean it?" I asked.

"Yeah. Absolutely," he said.

I thanked him. Miguel and I walked along the boardwalk for a while and sat on a bench facing the ocean. And ate.

"He really liked your story, Swee' har!"

I looked at the people leaning against the railing on either side of us, holding their fishing rods, or re-baiting their hocks. Then I looked out at the ocean.

This is where I sold my first story, I thought. And this is the first stage I acted on.

5.5

The regular beach and the nude beach
were separated by a huge rock
you had to climb over.
When you got to the nude side,
The same old Pacific ocean rolled ashore.
On the opposite side of the beach
was a tall cliff that flattened out at the top
and became a road and a town.
Young men in dark clothes sat along the top of
the cliff, their legs hanging over the edge,
and looked down at the naked women lying
on the beach
or walking along the ocean.
One of the naked men on the beach yelled
up to them.
"Hey perverts! Come down here to the beach
or go away! Assholes!"
But none of the men at the top came down.
Or went away.

And the naked men on the nude beach
didn't climb up.
One of the men at the top sat so close to the edge
he fell.
His body bounced against the dirt and stones
as he tumbled down the cliff.
When he hit the sand at the bottom,
He lay still, his arms and legs all twisted up.
People went over but didn't know what to do.
Someone at the top must have run to a building
and called for help.
In a little while, helicopters came
and took him away.
Naked people and the ocean were the last things
he ever saw.

6
Home Box Office

I hadn't been in Los Angeles very long when I talked to my mother, in Connecticut, on the phone and she told me that the woman who baby-sat me when I was a baby there in New Britain, long ago, was now living in the San Fernando Valley and was a TV producer. I was skeptical that my old babysitter could help my acting career, but I wasn't about to ignore the possibility. I called her. She said, "Come over." I did.

"Look at you!" she said when I found her house. "I haven't seen you since you were in diapers! Oh my God! You got so big! So, what are you doing now? Visiting?"

"Well, I was living in Maine and I got divorced so I thought I'd come out here and become an actor. Darrell let me stay with him for a while and get settled and then I got my own apartment."

"I see. An actor! Wow! Were you an actor in Maine?"

"No. I drove a school bus."

"Uh huh. Did you ever act – anywhere?"

"I was in a play in High School. The Seagull. By…"

"Anton Chekhov, if I'm thinking of the right Seagull," she said.

"Yes, that's the right one," I said.

"Okay. So. Not a *lot* of experience. But I guess people have done more with less. You do have a certain look. Are you taking acting classes now," she asked.

"Well, I met someone who is sort of managing me now and he had me get into a class with Stella Adler. So, I'm studying with her," I said.

"Oh wow. She's the best! So, you are doing good stuff. Do you like Stella?"

"Yes. She talks a lot about Marlon Brando and how she knew he would be a star the minute she met him. I keep waiting for her to say she knows I'll be a star, but she hasn't yet. She probably didn't tell Brando he'd be a star when she met him, either." I'm sure she could tell I was kidding. A little.

"Yes, you're probably right," she said, with a smile. "So, look, I'm assistant producing a show for a new TV company called HBO. The show is a tribute to the old vaudeville people who used to travel around the country, acting in live theatres. I need some people to be part of some background groups and maybe do some heavy lifting. Danny Devito and George Burns and a lot of old-time vaudevillians are going to be in it. Are you interested?"

"That would be so fantastic!" I said. "Really? I would love to!"

"It will be fun," she said. "George Burns is getting kind of old. He's in his early 80's now, but he's the best. And, you know who Danny Devito is?"

"He's the star of 'Taxi', right?" I asked.

"Yes. That's him. You've seen the show?"

"Yes, sure. Funny! And George Burns! I can't believe it!"

We went out to her back yard and talked some more. She wanted to know what I'd been doing the last 25 years or so, and I filled her in on my life. It didn't take that long. I'd quit high school when I was 16 but then went to a kind of progressive high school in Massachusetts, graduated and went to college for a semester and quit and then worked at a housing project, got married, lived in Maine and drove a little school bus, got divorced and quit driving, then came here, to California.

She nodded a few times and then said, "Interesting." That was a big word in Los Angeles. People said "interesting" a lot. It showed interest, of course, and appreciation, and respect, and could be said after almost anything someone told you. For instance, I could tell someone I used to unclog sinks with a long electric plumber's snake, and all the person listening to me had to say in reply was, "Hmm, interesting." Or if someone told me that she broke her leg two years ago while skiing in Utah, and it took forever to heal, all I had to say was, "Hmm, interesting." No one really expected more or wanted more.

There were rehearsals for the HBO Show. The dancers and burlesque people were all professionals who worked in Las Vegas night clubs and hotels and casinos. The comedians had all spent decades entertaining adults all over the country with adult jokes and sketches. One sketch in the HBO show was about a woman, described in the script as "well endowed," who fainted at a circus. Someone knelt beside her and held her head off the ground. Other men came over to help. One guy yelled to the man holding her head up, "Rub her arms. Rub her <u>arms</u>!" Another guy yelled out, "Rub 'er forehead. Rub 'er <u>forehead</u>!" Then this guy in a clown suit walked by holding a big collection of colorful floating items, yelling, "Rubber Balloons! Rubber Balloons! Come and get 'em! Rubber Balloons!"

During one of the rehearsals my old babysitter put me in a new sketch. All I had to do was walk in line with other extras who walked, diagonally, from one side of the stage to the opposite side. After we had rehearsed it a couple of times my old babysitter told me that it would be better if I wasn't in this sketch.

"Am I too tall or something," I asked.

"No, not really," she said. "It's just that when everyone else walked across the stage, they put their right arm in front of them and their left arm behind them. Like people do. Then they moved their left arm out in front and their right arm went behind."

"Oh," I said. "I didn't do that?"

"No," she said. "When you walked across the stage, first you put your right <u>and</u> left arms out front, at the same time, and then you put your right and left arms behind. At the same time. It was a little...unusual."

I had to laugh, imagining what I looked like. But she did put me into two scenes that I hold dear. One was a scene where I was sitting at a bar counter, and Danny Devito was the bartender behind the counter. The camera was behind me and focused on him, of course, but everything he said, he said to me. You could see my profile when the camera moved one way or another to capture Devito pouring coffee into my cup or putting the coffee pot back down on the burner. He talked to me about acting, and how it took forever to actually get a job, and how in the meantime, a time that could last for years, or forever, coffee was about all you could afford to order. If you were lucky.

"It could take you a long time to get a job, kid," he said. "So, I hope you like coffee. You're going to drink an awful lot of it."

I think I nodded my head once or twice while he talked, to show that I was listening, and that I was a good actor. Maybe he would see that I was a natural and when the scene was over, he'd ask if I wanted to be in a show of his. Something like, "Hey kid. Good nodding! You really know how to improvise. That's a gift! I think I can find something for you in my next show. I'll give you a call." It helped a lot in those days to be impossibly optimistic.

My last scene didn't give me a chance to show off my acting skills as much, but I loved it anyway.

"Fred," my ex-babysitter/director said, "I'm going to put you in this Arabian dance scene. You are going to wear these fluffy silk pants. You'll have no shirt on, and you are going to carry a woman who is rolled up in a rug onto the stage and *gently* lay her down. When the rug is on the floor, you will pull until the rug is unrolled and the woman inside tumbles out. Then she rises and begins dancing and you exit stage-left. Sound okay?"

"It sounds perfect because both my arms do the same thing at the same time."

"Right! You can handle it. You just lay the rolled-up rug on the floor, pull on the end of it until the rug is all un-rolled and the woman appears. Then she gets up and dances and you get your ass out of there."

"I think I can do that!" I said.

The smile she gave me was tinged with worry.

"Now remember," she said. "This woman will be naked, except for a little foo-foo on her pooh-pooh. So don't stand there staring at her. By the time she gets up to dance, you should be halfway to the exit. Okay?"

"Sure," I said. "Unroll her and leave. Got it."

"And when you walk away, remember, one arm to the front and the other to the rear, back and forth."

"Of course," I said.

The night of the taping, all went smoothly. We had to do the scene a few times, but not because of me. There is always something a director wants to change. And after each time I walked off stage proudly, hands alternating left to right, the gorgeous woman standing up from the rug and beginning to dance, beautifully naked, except for the little foo-foo on her pooh-pooh.

6.5
Ann Margret

My old babysitter/new producer called me after
the HBO Vaudeville Show was over and
she asked if I'd like to be in the
n*ext* HBO show.
"It's an Ann-Margret Special," she said.
"Of course, I would!" I said.
"Roger Moore plays Rhett Butler
and you will play his double
in the 'Gone with the Wind' scene."
While on the show,
I met Mr. Moore and Ann-Margret
and worked with them and
I spoke a little Swedish with Ann's mother
and made her laugh.

The hoop skirt under Ann's petticoats in her
Scarlett O'Hara costume
was so heavy,
circled so far out from her body,
that she had to lean back against a wooden stand
while the costume ladies tied
and buttoned her outfit together.
The hoop lifted from the ground at an angle,
into the air,
as Ann leaned further back.
Roger Moore walked by, stopped,
and looked her
up and down
and under, and said,
with his lovely English accent,
"Ann dear, they've forgotten your knickers."

Story 7
Early Call

Carl, the owner of the travel agency, was so proud of himself when he sold his business to a group of men and bragged to me that he was still the "overall owner." I had been working there for over four years, still not sure about how to record all the bills they put on my desk and how to make sure they all got paid, but I was still able to go on auditions when I needed to and take days off if I happened to get a part on a show, which I did from time to time.

"What's an *overall owner*?" I asked, as we walked along the bottom floor of the triangle buildings to get some coffee.

"What are you talking about?" Carl asked.

"You said they bought the business, but you are still the overall owner."

"Oh. It means I have final say on everything," he said. "They run the place and can hire and fire, but I am still the main owner."

"Uh huh. Can *you* fire *them*," I asked.

"Fire them? Well, uh…Fire them? I…Uh…"

Within a few months the new owners had sold a whole bunch of cruise tickets to faraway places and then kept the money. The cops were looking for them, and a cruise liner

42

full of travelers to the far East were dumped on an island in the Philippines with no food or shelter because the new owners never sent the cruise company the money to pay for the tickets. And Carl, who thought he was still the owner of the company, was now broke.

Fortunately, the new people had fired me weeks before the company went bankrupt. I like to think they probably figured I was on to them and didn't want me around. I started my own yard-care business. I called it "Quiet Tools," because since I couldn't afford any motorized tools, like a gas-powered lawn mower, all my tools *were* quiet. I bought myself an old pick-up truck that usually ran okay, and a push mower and a few hand tools, and started driving around Los Angeles taking care of peoples' yards. Fran, my wife-to-be in a couple of years, left her commercial artist job about that time and we worked together. We charged ten dollars an hour and we split it evenly.

Five dollars an hour doesn't seem like much these days, and it wasn't much then either, but Darrell had introduced me to a man, who was probably a patient of his, from France, who had an avant-garde men's clothing store and he needed someone to take care of his yard. He had a single-family house on a road full of single-family houses owned by well off, but not really rich people, and there was a guest room below the main floor and he said I could live there. The guest room was really a small apartment with a kitchen and bathroom and a large living room/bedroom, all for free if I mowed the lawn and watered the plants.

One morning the phone rang, and it was Darrell's old girlfriend from a few years ago, the realtor, who had lived with him until she found the house he bought. I told you she would show up again. She wasn't selling real estate anymore. Now she worked for one of the free magazines that were all over LA along the sidewalks, in scratched plastic boxes sitting on metal legs. You could just pull open the door and take one. There was some information in them about things happening in town, but mostly there were ads from all kinds of people looking for all kinds of other people, sometimes for friendship and lots of times for very intimate and/or very strange activities.

I answered the phone.

"Hi Fred! It's Darrell's old girlfriend, Dana. Remember me?"

"Hi! Of course! How are you?"

"I'm fine. Listen – I'm at work so I can't talk long, but there is an ad in the magazine I work for now and I thought of you. It's for a movie the new Playboy Channel is making. Come to my office if you are interested and I'll connect you with someone in charge of the auditions. What do you think?"

"Wow! Sure! I'd love to! Any special time or day?"

"Well, the sooner the better. Can you come tomorrow at about 11:30? I'll have some time then and we can talk. Okay?"

"Yes! Great! I'll see you tomorrow!" She gave me some directions and the next day I was at her desk at 11:30. We hugged and said how good we both looked and then I sat next to her desk.

"Coffee?" She asked.

"Oh, no thanks. I just had some."

"So here is the ad. I'm friends with the woman who wrote

it. You just go to this office, and I guess it's like an audition."
She told me where the office was and then gave me a copy
of the thin magazine. "Do you know how to get there?"

"Sure. It's not far from where I used to work. I'll head
right over!"

I thanked her for thinking of me and took off for the
building about three miles away where they were holding
auditions. I expected to see a long line of people waiting
there, as usually happens when no agents are involved and
anyone could show up for an audition, but hardly anyone
was there waiting to be seen.

There was the usual waiting room with a secretary at
her desk and a door that led to the room where the auditions happened. I was given a script to read until it was my
turn to audition. Just a page and a half. Something about a
rich young man meeting his girlfriend in the forest so her
husband wouldn't find out.

"Hi, Fred," The casting agent said when I went into her
room. "Welcome. So you know Dana, huh?"

"Hi. Yes. She was living with my brother when I came
to California a few years ago."

"That must have been Darrell, right?"

"Yes. So you know Darrell, too?"

"Mostly just what Dana has told me. Seems like a good
guy. By the way, I'm Jen. Okay, let's get down to business.

So, I'll read the woman's part. Her husband is a rich man
who travels a lot, and when he is gone, she meets up with
her boyfriend, who is much younger than her husband. The
story is called "The Tale of the Toe" because the wife ties a
string to her toe every night then throws the string, with a

little stone tied to the end, out her second-floor bedroom window. Her boyfriend picks up the string. If the husband is in bed with her, she pulls the string up and her boyfriend goes away. But if her husband is not home, she takes the string off her toe and throws it out the window. That means she'll be right down. That's why it's called "The Tale of the Toe." It was written by Boccaccio hundreds of years ago."

"A real classic," I said, and then wished I hadn't.

"Absolutely. Okay, let's start."

Jen read the young wife's part and I read the young man's. The other woman filmed the audition. It took about five minutes.

"Thank you," Jen said. "Say 'Hi' to Dana for me."

"Sure," I said. "Nice to meet you." As I went back outside, I thought, "This will never happen."

7.5
Dana at Darrell's

Dana was up on the newest styles
in the late 70's.
Sometimes, when she still lived with Darrell,
I'd see her on the floor,
with her legs up in the air
at a right angle to her body,
pulling as hard as she could
to make her jeans slide down
from her feet to her waist,
so she could stand up and zip them
and go about her business.
"Jeans have to be tight," she'd say.

Story 8
The Mansion

Two weeks went by. Fran and I had been going out every morning and raking yards and pruning bushes and mowing lawns, as usual. The audition for Playboy's "Tale of the Toe" went out of my mind, mostly, just as other auditions I never heard from again also went out of my mind. And then the phone rang early one morning. I got out of bed and answered.

"Hello…"

"Hello. Mr. Burstein?"

"Yes. Yes, this is Fred."

"Hi Fred! I'm calling to tell you that shooting for the "Tale of the Toe" will begin this coming Wednesday. Can you be at the Playboy Mansion at 8 AM that day?"

"Playboy Mansion? Yes. Sure! Absolutely! Thank you! Should I come by for the script?" I asked.

"You won't have to. The script is on its way to you right now. It will be left at your door in a little while," the lady said. "It might even be there now."

I said to myself, They are *bringing me* the script! "Oh. Great! I'll be there Wednesday. And thank you!"

"You are very welcome. And congratulations! See you at the mansion!"

I hung up the phone (this was 1982) and stood there quietly. I let the words bounce around in my brain so I could enjoy them for a while. Then I got into the old truck and went to get Fran so we could mow and prune and plant with our quiet tools all around Los Angeles. I couldn't wait to tell her.

I got to the mansion bright and early on Wednesday. I'm not sure if I pedaled my bike or drove my old pick-up truck. Either way, people were probably surprised when they realized I was there to act in the movie and not to deliver a package, maybe peacock food (there were a lot of peacocks walking around).

Making the twenty minute 'Tale of the Toe' was going to take two days. I was paid five hundred dollars a day and there would be no royalties, no matter how many times the show was aired. And even though the 'Tale of the Toe' was probably aired over a thousand times that first year, I didn't mind not getting paid any royalties. I still don't.

The Playboy Mansion was more like a medieval castle than a huge house. It was all stone and had a tower or two that might have had soldiers standing in them armed with bows and arrows guarding the place. It was crazy. Outside there were acres of lawn decorated with flowers and marble statues and fruit trees.

A thin, man-made brook ran all through the lawns, flowing around and around the Playboy property endlessly. The peacocks walked here and there, many with their tails spread out behind them in a show of masculinity.

I was brought to a room to meet my co-star, who was that year's Miss July. She was young, ("I just turned 18!" she blurted out with her arms raised in triumph and a big smile on her face). She was energetic and in constant motion. We went over the script and the settings for a few hours with the other cast members and then took a lunch break. There were tables full of food for us, and I had time before the next rehearsals to use the shower-house near the famous pool, where naked Playboy models swam and sunned as I lived and breathed.

After I got dressed, Miss July, Lynda Wiesmeier, came running out of somewhere towards me, without any clothes on, and jumped up and locked her legs around my hips and her arms around my neck. "I *love* being naked!" she said. "I wish I was naked *all the time*!"

Most of the scenes in the movie happened at night, so while we waited for it to get dark, we rehearsed some more. In one scene I was to meet Lynda outside her character's home and take off her nightgown and hug and kiss her.

No one told me to take the night gown off *very* gently, as if it was worth thousands of dollars. Which it was. I thought it would be appropriate and theatrical if I ripped the damn thing off and *then* gave her hugs and kisses.

When I started to rip the gown to shreds, one of the staff watching on the side screamed out in horror, "St-o-h-h-hp! Oh my go-h-h-h-d! Don't move!" She ran over and frantically tried to put the shreds of the nightgown back together on Lynda's body. "That nightgown is a hundred years old!"

she blasted. "It's worth more than *you are*!"

I wanted to say, "*Now* you tell me." But I kept still and quiet, hoping she didn't send me home. She took Lynda away and dressed her in a newer, cheap nightgown that looked just as good as the expensive one, and now I could rip and tear to my heart's desire. But I was very careful with it.

In the evening we all headed for the game room on the property, where make-up and our 14th century costumes would be put on. The game room was a whole separate building, filled with genuine classic pinball machines, pool tables, antique player pianos, and other old-fashioned rare distractions.

We were all being changed into our 14th century ornate costumes and painted with brushes full of make-up when "Heff" came in, dressed in his signature red robe and slippers, probably smoking his pipe. He was surrounded by his henchmen who went around to all of us and explained that we had to leave and find another place to change and get made-up because it was "Heff's" game time. I felt like telling them that we were making *Heff's* movie, so couldn't he go somewhere else for one night? But I had already caused enough trouble, so I just followed the movie staff to a different location.

I was dressed in a gorgeous hat with tall white feathers that swayed when I walked, an enormous cape with a thin gold collar, and I had a shining silver sword at my side that went all the way down my silk black pants to my high black leather boots. Oh, I thought, if the kids who called me 'Dumbo' in 5th grade and asked me if I could flap my ears and fly, could see me now. Actually, maybe they did see me. When I was visiting my parents back home after the show had been on The Playboy Channel for a while, one of the kids I grew up with said to me, "Christ, Burstein. Every time I turn on the TV now – I have to look at your ass!"

The second night at the Mansion, the director came over to me after I had done a "take" of one of the most pivotal scenes in the show to give me some direction.

In the scene, I was supposed to go to my lover's house and then pull the string that hung out of her window. Her husband was home, and he had seen the string that went from her toe to the window and figured out what it was for! So, he gingerly takes the string off her toe and throws it out the window. Ah, I think, holding the end that had been around her toe, she will be down to see me soon and we will lie under the stars in each other's arms! So, I smiled and waited. But it wasn't my beautiful sweetheart who had come out to see me, but her old and bearded husband who came stomping out of the mansion, determined to kill me! That was my cue to turn around and run like hell. Which I did. But that's when the director yelled, "Cut!" and came over to talk to me.

"Look," he said. "How about when you are running away, you slow down a little and look back to see how close the husband is. Then I can get a good shot of your face. Smile maybe."

I said something like, "Sure!" and we began doing the

scene over. When the enraged husband came running toward me, I took off into the woods. But this time I slowed down, turned my head toward him and exhibited my acting talent by running backwards and looking at him with a smile on my face. As I ran so effortlessly backwards, I suddenly crashed into something ahead of me and it fell to the ground, and then **I** fell to the ground. I had smashed into a huge, ancient marble statue of a naked woman that stood beside the path.

I wasn't moving. Everyone panicked. The director and camera people and make-up people all came running over to me. The big question in their eyes was, Is he *alive*?

The director got down on his knees near my head. He leaned in and said, "Can you hear me?"

For a second I almost said, like Curly of the Three Stooges, "Soitenly!" But I took a breath, sat up, and said, "I'm okay," And then I stood.

They all exhaled with relief. Probably not so much because I wasn't dead, but because now they could finish making the movie without having to do it all over with a new actor, one who was alive, thus running the cost of production way, way out of control. How would they explain that to "Heff?"

Thank GOD!" The director said. "Okay everyone! Let's lift that statue up and get back to work! We are wasting time, people!"

Four or five men went over to the tall marble woman now lying on the ground and put their hands under her head and arms so they could lift her back up.

Someone said, "Okay, on three! One…two…three!" And they all heaved but the statue didn't move. "Okay, again!

One…two…three!" And again they all grunted and tried to lift the naked marble lady, but she wouldn't budge.

"Okay, leave her be!" the director said. "Let's *finish* this thing. They will have to get a crane in here to get her back up." He looked at me and said, "*Sure* you're alright?" It sounded like he was thinking that I couldn't possibly be alright, but…

"I'm fine," I said. "Sorry about…"

"No time for that now. Places everybody!"

The crew went back to their cameras and buckets full of make-up, shaking their heads in disbelief. Lynda Wiesmeier came over to me, in her less expensive but still soft and transparent ivory colored nightgown, and said, "I'm never, ever, coming *near* you again!"

But she did, and when we finished making believe we were making love, she stood near the fallen naked statue, dimly lit, happy it was all done, and that she was naked too.

8.5
Born Too Late

I wouldn't call myself a thief,
but I *did* steal a Playboy Magazine when
I was 13.
I would have bought it, but I was too young.
I stuffed it into the already fantastically thick
Sunday New York Times
at the tiny store near the beach,
and hoped no one would notice
that The Times had gotten a visitor.
Thank God, no one did.

9
Moving

Leonard was keeping a secret from me, and probably every-one else, and towards the end of the five years I had known him, he was becoming more and more depressed. He talked of killing himself. I thought it was because no one bought his screenplays anymore or maybe he was running out of money. He had been head writer in the 50's of the hit show "The Untouchables." He had written some B movies and a play that made it to Broadway for a short period of time and he wrote episodes of a lot of other shows in the sixties and early seventies, including "The Streets of San Francisco" and "The F.B.I." But by the time I met him in 1977, and after, no one was buying his scripts anymore. He was still able to pay the rent for his Mustang convertible and his apartment, but I worried that he'd be broke soon. Or broken.

Leonard's Twilight Zone friend, James, told him that he should go back to New York City, because he grew up there and liked it much more than Los Angeles, and see if he had better luck wanting to live and work there. If he still felt terrible in New York, he could kill himself. But not yet. So Leonard took that advice and moved to New York City and lived in a one room apartment on the Upper East Side that his sister owned on 82nd Street. I stayed in Los Angeles and got the job on The Playboy Channel and soon after that I was cast as the lead horse (really) in a small production of "Equus" that would be performed on a small stage in Burbank, California

The lead horse didn't have any lines, but it had a huge metal horse head made of welded together thin metal rods that sat on my shoulders and rose way over my head. I wore no shirt, but I had pants on this time, unlike during half the scenes in "Tale of the Toe." One of the perks of being the lead half-naked horse was that I would be near the teenage lovers when they took off all *their* clothes and got together on the floor. I think I was supposed to make horse sounds while they were at it. But I left the play before any of that happened.

While I still was part of the cast, the people putting the show together held some very suspicious auditions behind closed doors. They called in a bunch of young women for the girl's part, and the girls had to read something from the script and then take off their shirt and bra, if they wore one. The two lovers were naked during a scene in the play, so the producers, I guess, had to make sure the girl had breasts. Of a certain kind. They took nothing for granted. The young man who played the young man was also one of the producers, so he sat in on all the many "take off your top" auditions. In the end, none of the young women who auditioned and went into the secret room to read some of the script and then let the judges stare at their naked breasts were chosen for the part. The young producer/lead actor chose his own girlfriend for the role.

I never saw any of the undress-rehearsals nor any of the actual play, and I never got to walk around with my giant metal wire horse head looming over my naked torso, because before any of that could happen Leonard called me from New York and said, "Stop what you are doing – and come to New York."

9.5
Leaving L.A.

I met some friends at Joe Allen's
before I flew to New York.
We sat outside under the flame heaters on posts
and had a beer and some nachos
and said "Good-bye."
For years I thought of living in Los Angeles
as a sacrifice I made to become an actor,
but by the time I had to leave,
I loved it.
It had become my home.

10
New York

Leaving Los Angeles turned out to be the best thing for Leonard. At least in the beginning. He became the head writer for the soap opera "The Doctors" not long after he got to New York. There was a nationwide Writer's Strike at the time with writers asking for proper pay and new rules for the new inventions of "pay TV" and home video. Most union writers didn't work during the strike, but Leonard was offered the job and he decided to take it. I think he changed his Writer's Name so his union membership wasn't known. He was angry and suicidal. He hadn't been offered a job in years. The union seemed to have forgotten him, so he decided to be a scab. And maybe he knew, either consciously or unconsciously, that he only had a few more months to live. I had no idea that he was battling diabetes. He never said a word. And he had never told me that his father had died of diabetes a long time ago. He might have known that he didn't have much time left, so, *union-shmoonion*. If I want to stretch things a little, I could say he might have wanted to set me up with a good job before he left me and the world.

In addition to overseeing and writing the new scripts, the producer of "The Doctors" wanted Leonard to write a new character for the show. Leonard made the character fit me as much as he could. The show was low in the ratings, and this was a last ditch effort to save it. Leonard and the show were dying at the same time. After Leonard called and told me to come to New York, I left the "Equus" rehearsals and flew across country. Fran took over the Quiet Tools landscaping business. We figured I would either be back in California soon if I didn't get the job or I'd be staying in New York if I did. After I was in New York for about an hour I knew I wasn't going back: job or no job. Not that I loved New York so much. It was that I felt I had made progress, and I didn't want to mow lawns in Los Angeles any more. I had been mowing lawns for most of my life. I would ask Fran to come to New York too.

The character I auditioned for was a made-up famous football player who had been in a car accident and was in the hospital with his face completely torn to pieces and completely wrapped in gauze. I imagine the character's face went through the windshield. No other part of the character's body was injured. I was put in my outfit before the audition, which seemed semi-familiar to me by now: no shirt, no shoes, hospital short-shorts, and bandages hiding my whole face except for my eyes. A cast member, sitting in a chair waiting for some make-up, looked at my chest, raised his eyebrows and blurted out, "Holy shit! His tits are bigger than mine!" That young man was Alec Baldwin. "The Doctors" was his first job.

Alec had been on the show for a couple of years at that point, but he was fired soon after I met him in his second year because he was growing his beard again – for the 3rd

time. The producer told him he couldn't keep growing and then shaving his beard, and he would be fired if he didn't get rid of this new beard, so Alec ended up getting fired. He left the show with a bang, being shot by three different people all at the same time, all for different reasons, and all from different windows.

I met Alec again not too long after we both left "The Doctors" when I went to an audition for a part in the soon-to-be made TV mini series "Dress Gray." Alec was leaving the building, having just auditioned. He said hello and asked me how I was doing and wished me well with the audition in a friendly way, and then headed off somewhere. I thought to myself, "So sad. He has no chance whatsoever of getting this part, though he must think he has. Maybe he won't ever get any part. It's a shame because he's a nice guy." Could I have been any more wrong? He not only got the part, co-starring with Lloyd Bridges and Hal Holbrook, but he did a great job and became a huge star of stage, screen, and TV, as most of us now know.

There were several other actors auditioning for the same part I was trying to get on "The Doctors." Some who were well known. Leonard told me he did what he could to make the audition scene match who I was, but he told me there were several people who would decide who got the part, including the show's producer. After my audition I was told that no one would need me to be at the studio for at least a few hours, so I put on my street clothes and took off on a walk around the City. It was a warm, late summer day, and I walked across Central Park without even knowing I was headed for what was called the East Side. The Park looked beautiful, and I wandered around like someone who didn't know there were dangers there, especially in the early 1980's. I strolled and rested and looked around for about an hour when two people from "The Doctors" studio came running over to me.

Oh my god, what are you doing out here!" one of them asked.

"They said I should take off for a couple of hours after my audition. So I went for walk."

"Well, they want your ass back! Now! You have a second audition! Run!"

So, I ran, auditioned a second time, and was sent home, which, for the time being, was my brother Bobby's apartment in Brooklyn Heights. I sat around waiting for a call from Leonard.

Eventually the phone rang and after I answered and said "Hello," a man's deep voice said just one word to me – "Yes."

10.5
Cab Ride

Leonard and I stood by the side of the road
to hail a cab.
We were going out to eat to celebrate.
For a while all the cabs that went by
had passengers.
I had learned recently that if a cab
can pick you up,
the lights on their roofs will be on.
Finally, a cab with its light on stopped next to us
and we got in.
We almost got right back out,
but the lady driving the cab took off too soon.
"Where to, boys?" she asked.
We looked around.
The floor in the back looked like
it was used to haul garbage.

The driver looked like a homeless woman
who had high-jacked the cab from the real cabbie
and then stopped for us.
We told her the address of the restaurant,
looked at each other,
and raised our eyebrows.
We both understood that we might not
ever see the restaurant,
or anything else ever again!
Then the driver asked us,
"Do you boys know Dover?"
"Dover?" I asked.
"Yes," she said. "Dover.
You know, Dover is Over!"
Then she drove a little while and repeated,
"Dover – is – <u>Over</u>!"
She laughed and we laughed too,
beginning to enjoy this theatre of the absurd.
Leonard asked, "Dover is…over?"
"<u>Yes</u>," she repeated.
"D<u>o</u>ver – is – <u>O</u>-ver!"

A head shot I used after "Ryan's Hope" taken
at my house in Kerhonkson in 1987

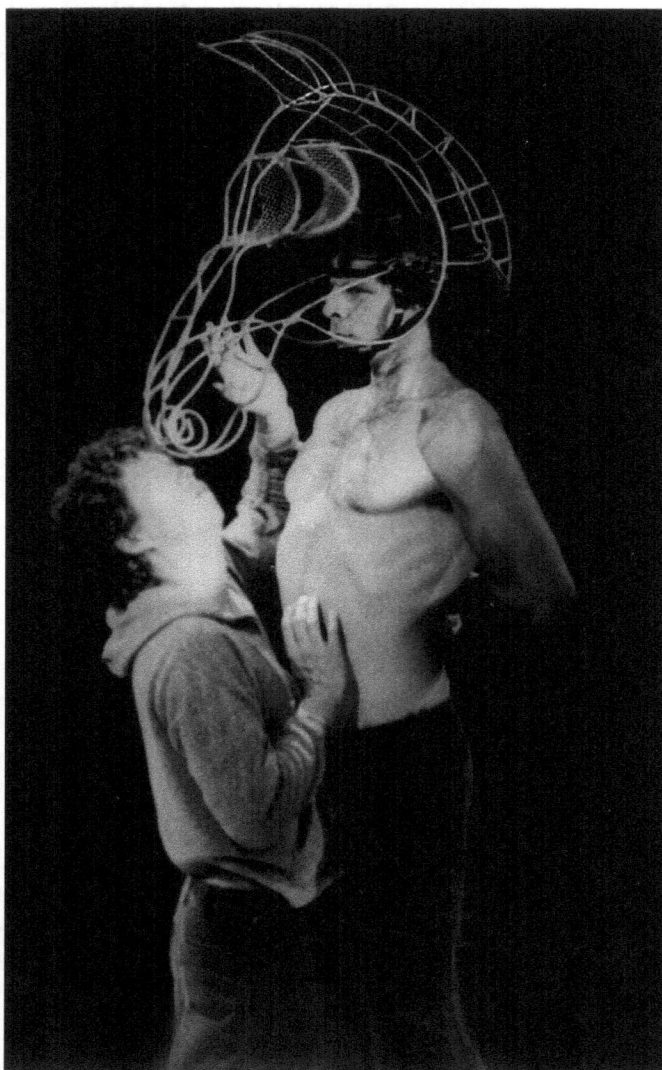

Rehearsal for *Equus* in Los Angeles
just before I left for New York
to work on *The Doctors* in 1982

Joe Hardy and I on a trip to Paris in 1989

Anna, me, and Rebecca
still in Brooklyn Heights, NY in 1985

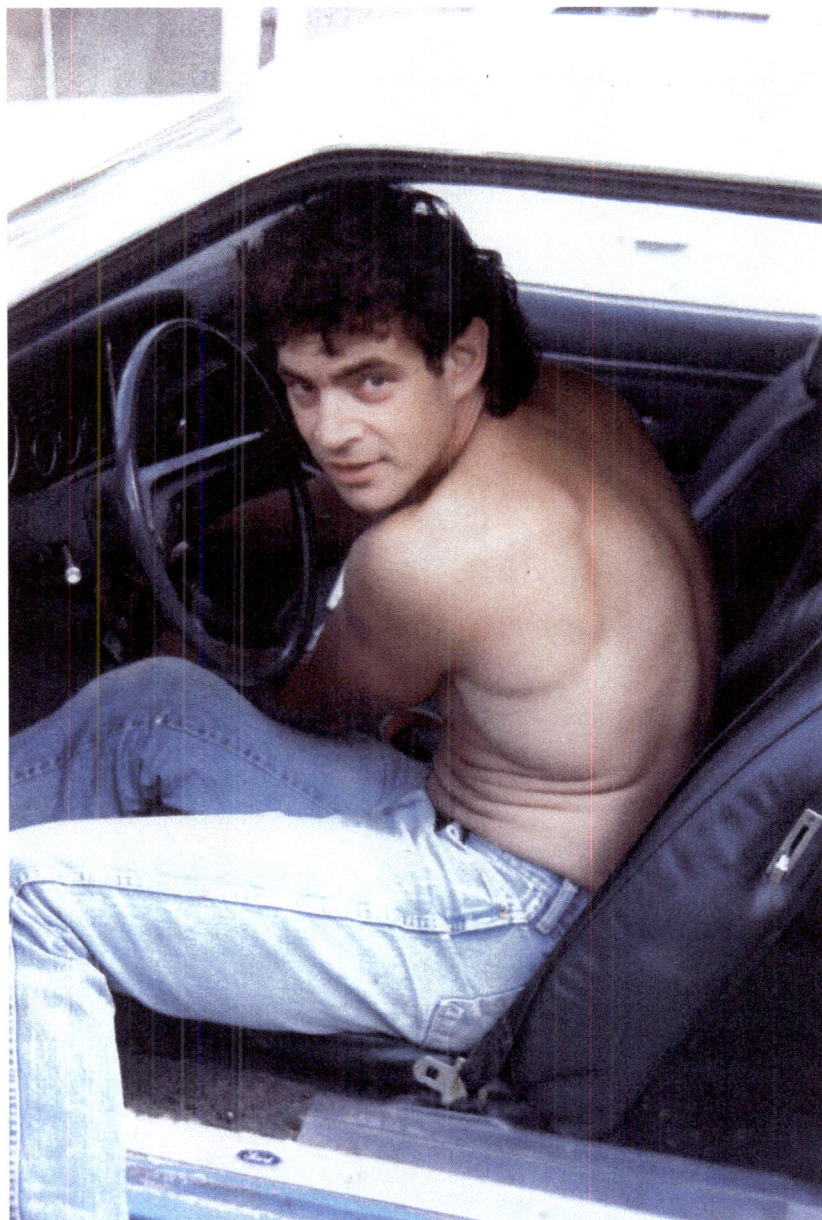

Trying to start the old Mustang when we first moved
to Kerhonkson, New York in 1986

Fran holding Anna on a visit to my parents' house
in New Britain, CT in 1985

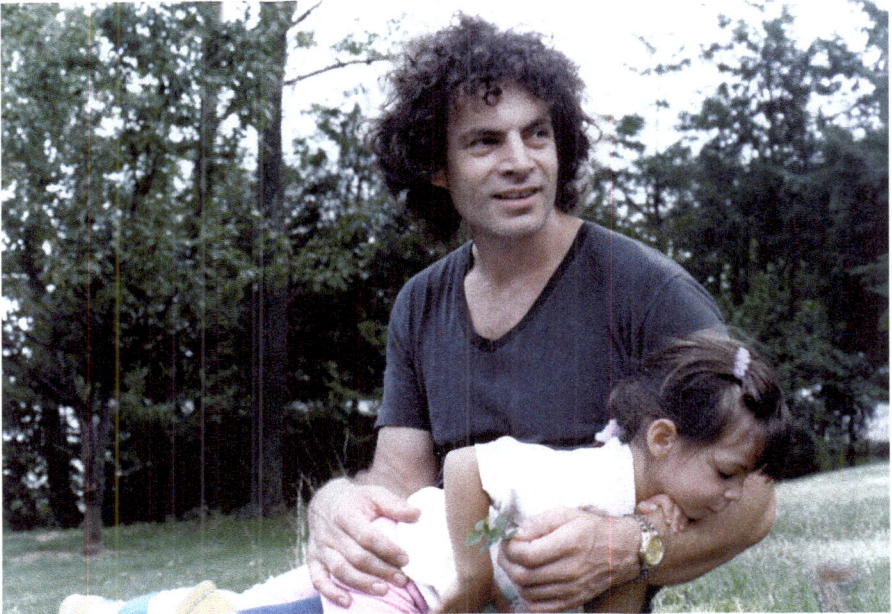

Anna and me in New Britain,
at my parents' house in 1988

Anna, Rebecca, and me after a year in Kerhonkson, 1987,
on the tire swing I made for them that hung
from our walnut tree.

Fran, Anna, and Rebecca at my parents' (Danny and Judy), place in Palm Beach, FL in 1989.

Anna and Rebecca with me at Joe Hardy's house doing some yard work in the wheel barrow I still use almost 40 years later.

Anna and Rebecca, happy in the sandbox at our house
in Kerhonkson, NY, about 1988

On vacation in Old Saybrook, CT, in 1990

1986, getting ready to hit the heavy bag
at the Gym in NYC

11
The Doctors

Working on "The Doctors" was sometimes fun and sometimes a pain. Like most jobs, I guess. One of the most often used directors had a strange way of trying to get the best out of the actors, especially the new ones and even the "extras," who had small parts as nurses walking around the hospital or maybe as a visitor waiting to see a patient. Sometimes these "extras" said a few words and sometimes they were just background visuals. This director insulted them, told them they made him sick. He made them cry and run away.

I was one of his targets. He'd ask me things like, "Who told you you could act?" "Why are you here?" "Why do I have to work with people like you?" It was not helpful.

Sometimes I thought he probably only said those nasty things to people who were so good he thought they needed reining in. And sometimes I thought he hated me. Months later, when I was auditioning for a part at the *All My Children* studio, the producer told me I was highly recommended by this same director. I told her I was surprised since he made my life miserable.

For a while, *The Doctors* was also an actor's miracle for me: it was a steady job. For a while. I took the subway from my brother Bobby's apartment on Cranberry Street in Brooklyn Heights early in the morning and went to the studio in midtown Manhattan. I had a little dressing room where I could study my lines before the rehearsals and rest there for a while.

Bobby helped me memorize my lines at the apartment when he came home from his job as a lawyer in the City, and he was always shocked at how long it took for me to learn them. I had read that Richard Burton could go over a script once and he would remember all his lines, and probably everyone else's too. It amazed me, especially since I could go over my few lines a dozen times and still not remember them. Burton could stuff "Hamlet" into his brain just by reading it once, so they say. Bobby knew all my lines after going over the script once or twice with me, and found it hard to believe it took me forever to memorize them.

I knew that it was not good that it was so hard for me to learn my lines. If you know your lines, you can concentrate on being the character and interacting with the other people in the scene. If you barely know what words come next, it is difficult to be totally engaged in the scene.

Since my face was always covered in bandages on the show, I was never recognized on the street in real life, but that was okay. I was thankful to be working, even if I had to endure nasty barbs from the director and spend hours to learn a few lines.

My character on the show had two main concerns. One was getting my torn-up face sewn together well enough so I could play football again without having parts of it fall off during the game. My other concern was: Did my nurse love *me* as much as I loved *her*? Everyone falls in love on a Soap. One day on the show I was lying in my bed, as usual, with my head and face (except for my eyes), all wrapped and taped, no shirt, no blanket, in my short pajamas, and my nurse came in to see me. I was supposed to tell her, now, that I loved her. Something made me think the best way to do that was to be direct and strong. But calm. None of this "gee wiz, I don't know if I can actually say the words" stuff, for me. My character was used to being smashed day in and day out by huge men on the football field who were trying to kill him. I wanted this woman, my nurse, to know how I felt about her. So in a direct, even way, I said to her, calmly, "I think I love you."

Well! Oh — my — GOD! You would have thought my bandaged head had fallen off and bounced on the floor and hit the director. He yelled, "CUT! CUT!! For the love of GOD, CUHHHHHT!!"

The nurse I "loved," *my* nurse, looked aghast, went off character, and hissed, "Are you kidding me?" I could tell she wanted to add the word "idiot" somehow.

And the camera people and make-up people turned their heads and looked away, probably trying not to laugh out loud.

The director said, "Hey! Knuckle Head! You are telling your nurse that you freaking *love* her – for Crys-sake! You aren't asking her for a cup of water! Put some goddamn feeling into it!"

I wanted to tell him, first of all, to shut the hell up. And then I wanted to tell him that the way I just told her I loved her was the *right* way. The strong way. But I knew I was just ahead of my time and he wouldn't listen to me. So we did the scene again and this time I stammered and hesitated, made shy, oh-gosh-can-I-say-this? faces, and looked away from her, and then at her, a few times when I told her that, well, yeah, gee, I loved her.

That worked for them.

I didn't think the show would last more than another month or two. And it didn't. The way my part was written, my main concern was: how I would *look* when my face was revealed. There was a picture of me on the wall behind my hospital bed that I had spent a full day posing for when I was first hired. I was naked (for a change) except for a towel that lay one way or another over my crotch as I stretched out on a couch with a big smile on my face.

That picture was a constant reminder to the audience of what my character wanted his face to look like when the bandages came off. I wish I could have made them change how much I cared about how I looked. It was embarrassing. Why would I give a damn what I looked like as long as I could still run and train and play football.

My character was a football player. I got smashed and pounded and piled-on and squashed by very heavy men while I lay on the ground after being tackled. At least, I shouldn't have been as obsessed about it as the writers made me.

The other scene that I still struggle with and dream of doing over, 40 years after the show went off the air, is my meeting, in my hospital bed, with Arthur Ashe. The show had invited celebrities to be in scenes to promote non-smoking. The only two of those celebrities I remember are Judy Collins and Arthur Ashe. Maybe they were the only two. I never met Judy Collins, but I did meet Arthur Ashe. He was, of course, the wildly popular tennis star and world respected advocate for peace and well-being.

However, when the producer of *The Doctors* asked him to come on the show, they weren't aware that he had something to do with promoting *Virginia Slims* cigarettes. I don't think they realized this until the day he came to do his anti-smoking scene, which had to be cancelled because of the *Virginia Slims*. But he was there, at the studio, and they had to do something with him, so they sent him to my hospital room, where the masked, half-naked football star could be his soap opera make-believe good friend, who would be happy to see him. And Arthur Ashe could make believe he came to visit an old buddy in the hospital. Which was all okay, I guess.

But the part that I keep trying to do over in my mind is what they had Arthur do as soon as he got to my room. Instead of standing at the door and saying something like, "May I come in?" or coming in and saying to me, "*Now* what the hell did you do?" and then, when I realized it was my old friend Arthur Ashe standing next to me, I would almost jump out of bed and give him a hug and tell my beloved nurse that, Oh my God!, this is my friend, *Arthur Ashe*, here, in my room! *The* Arthur Ashe, known the world over as a great sportsman and a great person!

But, no, that's not how it went.

What they had him do was come to my hospital-room door, stand there while the camera focused on him, and then say, "Hello, I'm Arthur Ashe."

WTF! I knew who he was. The whole *world* knew who he was! Who was he talking to?

"Hello, *I'm Arthur Ashe.*" Really?!?

I've tried a thousand times since then, October 1982, to go back in time and magically change how Arthur Ashe and I greeted each other when he ended up visiting *me*, because of a last minute change in the script, on the hospital set.

I haven't fixed it yet, but I'll keep trying.

11.5
Rosh Hashanah

Since I was in New York in 1982, working on "The Doctors," I went home to New Britain, Connecticut to go to my old Temple, with my parents, on Rosh Hashanah in September.

Rosh Hashanah was always one of the
hottest days
of the summer.
In a suit in the Temple, with hundreds of others,
many I'd known since we were all kids,
sweating and praying the service would end soon.
But it never did.
Finally, we all left the temple
And hung around on the sidewalk for a while.
Kids who weren't Jewish
walked past us, returning from school.
Kids at the Temple that I knew from way
back were
all grown up, some with their own kids.

We had gone to kindergarten at this Temple
together,
and later went to Hebrew School
three times a week
until most of us left after our
bar or bat mitzvahs, having had enough.
One of my old friend's father was there.
We used to go to his Shoe Store
on Main Street near the railroad tracks.
My mother took all four of us at the same time.
We'd hear the train whistle and yell "Train"
and run out of the shoe store
and we'd stand behind the safety bars that had
come down and blocked the tracks,
and watch the train pass and then we'd go back
to the store.
One or another of us would take forever,
Trying on shoe after shoe and saying
about each one,
"It's too small," or "It's too big,"
Until finally my exhausted mother would say,
"This pair is fine!
If you don't take it we are leaving anyway!"

So there he was, my old shoe salesman,
outside Temple after services.
Older, whiter hair, thinner.
He asked me how I was doing.
I said I was doing okay.
On a TV show in New York City,
called "The Doctors," I told him.
"That's nice," he said. "What do you play?"
"I'm a patient at the hospital because I had
a car accident."
"Ha!" he belted out. "Ha!
"You're not even a pretend doctor
on a show called – "The Doctors!"
I walked away, keeping
the word "asshole" from jumping out.

12
The Old School

Fran came to visit me from California towards the end of my time on the "The Doctors" in NYC. We took a ride to Lenox, Massachusetts because autumn, like every other season, is so beautiful there. And I wanted to show her my old high school, Windsor Mountain.

Public school in New Britain had started to make my head spin when I was a Junior. The year before, there were some teachers I loved: the award winning poet Constance Carrier who taught Latin and invited me to her room where we talked about poems I was writing; the science teacher who let me work on whatever I wanted in his class and talked freely to me about what he'd like to do with my very pretty young English teacher; and the English teacher herself, who found a way to walk sideways behind me in class and pretend she had to hop up and rub her ass across my back in order to get through the tight space between my seat and the desk behind me.

I quit public school in Connecticut in October of my Junior year because school made no sense to me anymore. I looked at the words in my schoolbooks and I couldn't read them. My father offered to read the books to me, but I couldn't listen. I wasn't willing to be yelled at by the teachers at school anymore either.

"Hey!" said the gym teacher, "get a haircut or I'll cut it *for* you!"

And I was getting a little detached from what my parents and others called reality.

I quit school and stayed home to write and I went to the library to get new books. But one of my parents' friends knew about a school, Windsor Mountain, in Lenox, Massachusetts; a small co-ed school of about 200 students. They said it was "liberal." We went to see it, and I decided to go there. It was a beautiful estate in the Berkshires on 150 acres of trees and lawns and views of far-off tree-covered hills. The Main House was a huge mansion built in 1905 for the lawyer and art collector Grenville Lindall Winthrop, who divided his time between Lenox and Manhattan. His huge art collection included works by Van Gogh, Winslow Homer, Renoir, Rodin, and William Blake, to name a few. Just before Mr. Winthrop died in 1943 (at the age of 78) he sold his Lenox estate to Max Bondy.

Dr. Bondy and his wife Gertrude, who were both Jewish psychiatrists who studied under Freud, had created a private high school in Germany but fled when Hitler came to power. First they moved the school to Switzerland, then to Vermont, then in 1943 they moved the school to Lenox. Max Bondy was the headmaster until he died in 1951, when his son Heinz took over.

The student body was diverse. There were children of famous musicians, actors, and writers. One student's father owned most of the taxi cabs in a huge American city. There were kids there like me, whose parents could just about find enough money to pay for tuition. And there were kids on scholarship whose parents hardly had any money at all. There were students from Africa and Asia, Puerto Rico and Canada. There were teachers and administrators who were World War Two heroes. There were young teachers who later became some of America's most respected writers and artists and inventors. There were students who became lifelong friends of mine.

I was able to choose the classes I wanted, so I never took math. In my senior year, when my parents came to the "Spring Parents' Weekend", they saw me play Boris Trigorin in Chekhov's The Seagull. I knew Sydney Poitier would be in the audience to see his daughter in the play, so of course I thought he would recognize my raw talent and invite me to be in his next movie, launching my career as an actor. My parents sat next to Mr. Poitier during the performance. He didn't contact me.

"He was *so* nice!" my mother said when we had dinner later. "He asked us if we knew of any good places to eat near the school and we mentioned a few places and he asked if we'd like to have dinner with him! I said that would be wonderful, but we weren't sure when you would be ready to eat and we didn't want to hold him up. I would be so nervous! Can you imagine?"

I told her that Harry Belafonte was somewhere in the play's audience too because his daughter was a student here, though she wasn't in the play. "Maybe we could have eaten with the Poitiers *and* the Belafontes, since they are friends and might be meeting for dinner," I said.

"Do you know his daughter!?" my mother asked, amazed.

"Oh, sure. We're friends," I said. "She broke her leg when she went hiking a few weeks ago and she's in a cast now. She asks me to carry her places all the time."

"Oh come on," my mother said. "*You* carry Harry Belafonte's daughter."

"Just sometimes," I said. "When she has to go up stairs or down a hill. Like, I carry her from one end of the dining room to the other so she doesn't have to use her crutches all that way. It's a long dining room. She's not that heavy. It's kind of fun."

"I'm sure," said my mom.

I became president of the Windsor Mountain student body in 1968, my senior year, which I had never expected. Neither had anyone else. Every night after supper all the students and all the teachers went to the auditorium, a short walk outside from the Main House. We walked down a narrow path hidden under huge evergreen trees that were probably planted by the crew of Mr. Winthrop. This night we were nominating students for the new school-president election. The student on stage conducting our meeting, the current student vice-president, wanted to be the next president. To be nominated, she had to leave the stage and be in the audience, according to Robert's Rules. She asked me to take the podium on stage so she could sit in the audience and be nominated. I went to the podium. She went to the audience. The first student I called on was supposed to nominate her, but he nominated me. Even though I was on stage. We didn't always obey Robert's Rules. When the election was held, I won.

By the time my senior year was over, I still had no idea what I wanted to do next. I knew I didn't want to go to college. The headmaster, Heinz Bondy, asked me if I would come back in the fall and be an assistant dorm father, so I did. My job was to live in the dorm and make sure all the kids were in their rooms for the night and didn't smoke.

I drove some students to the YMCA in near-by Pittsfield every week and showed them how to do some weightlifting, and I sat with my group of kids at my table every night for supper. Whenever we had meat for supper, one of the freshmen girls at the table needed my help to cut it. It was a little like trying to cut a new boot with a wooden knife.

One night there was a wild fight after supper between two boys over a girl. One of the boys was big for a 14-year-old and the other boy was small and thin for a 14 year old. When the girl said to the smaller boy that he was "too short everywhere," he lost his mind. He wanted to kill the other boy. He probably couldn't acknowledge that it was his girlfriend who had said it, since she probably knew the facts. He was so enraged and bent on fighting the taller boy that a doctor had to be called to the school that evening to give him a sedative. The doctor said the shot was strong enough to knock out an elephant.

But not this elephant. While I was watching over him that night, he woke up after a few hours, screaming like he was on fire as soon as his eyes opened. He tried to go outside to hunt down the boy who stole his girl. He kept repeating, "I'm going to kill him! I'm going to <u>kill</u> him!"

I kept him locked in my arms for hours until the other

teachers woke up and called the doctor back. This time he gave the boy an even stronger shot. Maybe strong enough to knock out a whale. I don't know where he was sent, but I never saw him at Windsor Mountain School again.

12.5
Heavy Snow

At High School in The Berkshires
sometimes it would snow so hard, so deep.
The snow fell thick enough to dull the
lights outside the Main House at night
as I walked back to my dorm.
Half way there, in the middle of the Main Lawn,
I'd stop, snow hitting my face and making me
shut my eyes,
then I'd lean back until I fell onto the
snow and lay
under the night sky.
I'd sink until I was hidden from anyone
who might walk by.
But no one ever did.
I'd consider staying there and freezing,
with the snow slowly burying me,
like I was in a sad Jack London story.
Then I'd stand up and finish my walk to the
dorm, the cries of wolves howling behind me.

13
Seafood Salad

"The Doctors" wrote me out of the show a few weeks after my post-surgery face bandages were taken off and everyone discovered that I looked like I used to look before my accident. The doctors had restored my face. Big surprise. The show itself only lasted a little longer.

My lawyer brother Robert got a new job near Boston and moved out of his apartment. He was kind enough to keep paying the rent for us. Fran left California and moved in. I was doing auditions again but until (hopefully) I got another acting job I had to get work somewhere so we could buy food and all that. I found a job in a small eatery that was called something like "Forks," or "Knives," that was on the Upper East Side, so I was able to see Leonard after work. He needed more help now , so I was glad the new job was close to his apartment so I could visit him often.

The eatery had some fantastic food, like a seafood salad full of curled octopus legs and slices of lobster. As I arranged the refrigerated glass display counter in the morning, I probably ate half the octopus and lobster pieces in the salads. It helped make up for the lousy pay I was getting.

One morning there was a woman outside the eatery

who seemed to be living in a world all her own. Her clothes looked like she had been wearing them since the first moon walk, without ever talking them off. She seemed to have no idea where she was or what she was there for. And instead of speaking, she looked around from place to place on the street, like a hawk, quietly being lost. One of the people I worked with, Lisa, said, "Let's bring her in and give her some food. Poor thing looks really hungry."

"The 'poor thing' looks really crazy," I said. "We should bring food to her out here. If you bring her inside no one else will come in. I don't think she'll really care, or know, if she's inside or outside."

"Oh come ohhhn," Lisa said. "I think it will make her happy to sit down inside and have something good to eat. Help me bring her in."

"Make her "happy", huh? Well, okay," I said.

Lisa took the quiet woman's arm and guided her inside to a table. "Wait here," she said to her. "Sit down honey and I'll bring you some food, okay?"

The woman looked around at the small interior and sat. My compassionate co-worker went to the display counter and got her a plate full of food: two slices of pork pate' with pistachios and dried cherries, a couple of buttered baguette slices, and some sparkling water. Probably some chocolate chip cookies too. The woman ate one thing after another, quietly, looking around, until it was all gone. Lisa watched with a smile on her face that grew bigger as the food disappeared.

Then the woman turned her chair, as if she were going to stand up and leave, but instead she opened her mouth and a stream of vomit flew out like water from a fire hose, parallel to the floor, until it just stopped, seemed to float for a second, and then fell to the floor in one piece.

Lisa and I looked from the vomit to each other, both of us horrified and amazed. Neither of us had ever seen anything like that in our lives. I still never have.

"What the Fuck!" Lisa said. "That shit flew five feet out of her mouth! Did you see that?!"

"Did I see it!? I'll probably see it for the rest of my life! And," I said, "I'm not cleaning it up!"

We guided the woman back outside and locked the door. With a snow shovel and a mop and a roll of paper towels, we scraped and scrubbed until the mess was gone. Then I opened one of the bowls in the refrigerated display counter and dug out a handful of octopus legs to cheer myself up.

13.5
Upper East Side(walk) Art

Weeks after the projectile lady left
I saw a crowd form in front of the little eatery.
A young woman, maybe 30, was standing
On the sidewalk outside the door.
Was this place a crazy magnet?
Dirt covered her skin like it had been painted on.
She stood still as people on the street
Kept their eyes on her.
Other than ragged pants, she was naked.
If her appearance alone didn't make you
walk away
You moved quickly when she pushed
her pants down to her bare feet, squatted,
and shit on the sidewalk.
Any people who were still watching
turned and ran.
Lisa was staring out from the open eatery door,
her mouth agape.
"Shall we invite her in?" I asked.
"Maybe she'd like to puke on the floor."

14
The Tip of Long Island

I'd been working for a while at the little "Forks" or "Knives" restaurant and going to Leonard's after work to help him with cooking and shopping. Once I went to get his pills. I took his Social Security card to prove to the pharmacist that I was getting the pills for Leonard, and I walked to the pharmacy, many blocks from the apartment. It took a while to get there and then a while to get back to him.

"What the hell took you so long!" he growled when I got back.

Well, it's a long way," I said.

Both his legs had been cut off above the knees by then, and he was miserable. The operations he had gone through and the medications he was taking had a terrible effect. He was getting more ornery and often told me I was a lousy cook when I made him something for supper.

A friend of his was at his apartment one night when I made some steak for all three of us in Leonard's little counter-top oven. Leonard took a bite and hissed, "This meat is *terrible*! It's over cooked! It's tough! Can't you even cook a steak!"

The friend told me that if Leonard talked to *him* like that after he had shopped and cooked for him, he would have walked out and stayed out for good.

"He's not really Leonard anymore," I said. "The real Leonard was taken away by his diabetes and the pills he's on and by the surgeon who cut off half his legs. He's really depressed. I mean, he can't walk or go anywhere alone or do anything without help."

"Yeah, I guess," his friend said.

"And he knows it's going to get worse," I added.

Leonard wanted to go to Long Island during that fall of 1983. He made a reservation at a hotel that was right on a quiet, out-of-the way beach so he could go on the deck in his wheelchair and be close to the ocean. Probably for one last time. After so much time in Los Angeles and Manhattan with him, I had no idea he loved being by the ocean. I drove him from the Upper East Side all the way to Montauk and helped him settle in. He was going to stay there for a few days, and then I'd come back to pick him up and take him home. Soon after I left him, still way out at the rural end of Long Island, I stopped at a roadside farm-stand and bought Fran a huge Blue Hubbard Squash.

The next morning I got an early phone call from the hotel that Leonard needed to be picked up right away. He had tried to get out of bed in the middle of the night and had tumbled to the floor. The caller said that when the housekeeper came to his room in the morning, she found him sprawled out near his bed, helpless and miserable after spending hours trying to reach the phone. I drove from Brooklyn to the end of Long Island again. I lifted him onto the front seat of the car and put the wheelchair in the back. I told him how sorry I was that he had such a shitty time.

"I couldn't go out on the deck," he said.

"How come?" I asked.

"When you open the sliding door, there's a metal frame that sticks up from the floor. I couldn't push the fucking wheelchair over it!"

"Christ!" I said. "You never got onto the deck! You lay on the floor all night! I'm really sorry. Next time there will be someone around to help you."

"There's no goddamn *next time*! I'll be dead soon and you know it," he said. "But…thanks for driving me out here. At least I could see the ocean from the bedroom – I could hear it."

We drove for a little while in silence. After a few miles Leonard said to himself, more than to me, "I wish I could die right now."

Leonard lived a few more months. Long enough to see the first few episodes of the new show I was on. He said I was doing a good job. When I went to the hospital to see him one day, he was barely alive. His eyes were open, but he wasn't seeing. He could hardly breathe. He didn't know I was there. I held his hand until a nurse took him back to his room. Then he was gone.

14.5
Welcome to New York

I was walking on the West Side in Manhattan
on one of the first days I was there
and I saw an old man and an old woman
screaming at each other.
They stood in front of a hotel with suitcases
at their feet.
They yelled louder and louder,
went back and forth with the ugliest words.
I didn't think it could get any worse
when the old man screamed,
"I only wish you would <u>die</u>!"
Rough town, I thought.
I had no idea.

15
Small Town
2/24/23 – 3 /3,4,5,13 /2023

Months after my job on *The Doctors* was over, I auditioned for and got a part on *All My Children*. I played a dentist who sold drugs, on the side, to wealthy people. The part was just a few episodes long, with the suggestion that if it went well, it could last a lot longer. I didn't have many lines, but the scenes were with main characters on the show. When I got my paycheck, I saw that I had been paid at the low "extra" rate. I thought I had enough lines in each episode so that I would be paid in the higher category of "visiting actor," or something like that. This all happened after Leonard went to The Hamptons and before he passed away. He was livid.

"You go see that producer and tell her that you were *not* an "extra." You had a regular part. You have to get paid more. Show her the script! You had a lot of lines! Show her some strength!"

So, like a fool, I did just what he said. And I *was* paid more money for those scenes. He was right! But I was never called back to *All My Children* again. At the time, it was devastating. As an actor, you always wonder if there will be a next job. For a lot of people, there wasn't, even after they were the stars of big shows.

"I'll quit TV and become a movie star," a lot of TV actors thought. Some did become famous and "movie stars," like Alec Baldwin, but many just quietly disappeared. I figured I was about to disappear very quietly and way before I became famous.

Walking in midtown Manhattan one day, maybe after an audition or while shopping for something that our new baby needed, someone called out. "Fred…?"

I looked around at the hundreds of people walking by. "It's George. George Baxt. Over here," the voice added.

I looked around again and found the man the voice came from. "George! Hi! What a surprise. What'chuh doing here in Manhattan?"

"I've more or less moved back here. Fuck Los Angeles. My publisher and my heart are here in New York. And my mother's here too, in the nursing home on 44th St., What the hell are *you* doing here? How did *you* end up walking in Midtown Manhattan?"

I used to see George Baxt in Los Angeles. He was a friend of Leonard's and we often ran into him at the "Joe Allen" restaurant in the evening. I hardly knew anything about George then, but I figured he had something to do with writing and show business and, like Leonard, I thought he wasn't doing as well as he used to do. He was smart and funny. I discovered a little later that he was the author of some wonderful books and had gotten some great awards. And would publish more books before his death in 2002.

"Well," I said, "you know, when Leonard came back to

Manhattan, *The Doctors* hired him to be its new head writer."

"Yes. He told me. But he didn't tell me you were here too."

"Well, at first I wasn't. He called Los Angeles one day and told me to come to New York for an audition at the show and I got the part. Then, you know, he was too sick to work any more, so he left the show. My part only lasted a few months. Then the whole show was cancelled."

"And now you are looking for a new show?"

"All the time," I said.

George found a pen in his coat pocket, tore off a piece of the New York Times he was carrying, and started writing. Handing me the paper, he said, "Call this number. My friend Joe Hardy is the Executive Producer of "Ryan's Hope." I'll tell him you are going to call and I'm sure he will see you. Do you have some tapes of your acting?"

"Yes," I said. "I have a tape of me on the Playboy Channel doing the short movie I made a little while ago and some tapes of me on *The Doctors*. And some earlier stuff."

"Okay, good. Give me a couple of days to get in touch with Joe, then you can call and make a date to see him. And bring your tapes. I'll tell him we are friends from back in Los Angeles and I'm sure he'll see you. More than that I can't guarantee."

"George…that's fantastic! Thank you! Can you write your number too so I can let you know how it goes? Maybe we can have a drink soon, like the old days at 'Joe Allen's.' "

"Here's my number," he said as he took the paper back and wrote it down. "There's a "Joe Allen" here too. We can meet after you talk to Joe Hardy and you can tell me how it went."

"I'll call you soon," I said. "I'm glad we ran into each other!"

"Yes," he said. "So am I. But it was bound to happen, you know. New York City is such a small town. I'll talk to you soon."

I don't always get what I wish for, but sometimes I do. As George went one way and I went another way, I felt that this unlikely crazy coincidental meeting was going to bring me somewhere really good.

15.5
The Train to Brooklyn

After meeting George I walked over
to the subway stairs
and went under ground
to wait for a 1, 2, or 3 train heading to Brooklyn
so I could go home.
A number 2 train slowed down and stopped
and I stepped into one of the open doors and
sat down.
Across from me was an African American man
sitting, quietly.
Standing to my side,
holding on to an over-head grab bar,
was a really tall, really big, African American man
staring at the man sitting across from me.
It seemed they were in the middle of something.
"Leave me alone, man. I don't want any trouble,"
the man sitting across from me said in a
soft voice.

The man standing to my side said,
"Fuck you, bitch. I'm coming for you."
The sitting man said again, still in a soft voice,
"Leave me alone man. I just want to get home."
I wouldn't want to fight
the man standing next to me either.
Then the tall man demanded, "Get up bitch!"
The sitting man said, "I just got out of jail.
But I'll go back if you don't leave me alone."
I thought, *He won't be able to go back to jail*
if this guy standing next to me kills him.
The standing man said, "Get up, mother fucker!"
The man across from me shot up,
pinned the tall man's neck against the grab bar,
pulled a knife from his pocket,
and held the blade against the tall man's neck.
It all happened in a second.
The tall man was scared to death
and begged the shorter man,
"Let me go. Don't do it. Please! Don't do it!"

The tall man's eyes opened so wide,
his face distorted with fear.
"Don't do it! *Don't* do it!"
The train was slowing down.
The shorter man thrust his knife
into and out of the tall man's side,
too fast to see.
As soon as the door opened, he was gone.
The tall man put one hand on the cut,
where blood spilled out,
probably glad his throat wasn't slit.
He kept saying,
"You just had to do it.,,
You just had to…"

16
Joe Hardy

I joined the cast of *Ryan's Hope* a little while after George Baxt spoke to Joe Hardy, the executive producer. Being on the show was a dream that lasted for two years, and the show stays in my mind these decades later. Joe Hardy and I are still friends. We did a lot together. We went to see the farm he grew up on in New Mexico. We went to the opera in Manhattan, to the theatre, and restaurants, and when he bought a weekend home in up-state New York, built in the 1800's on a narrow and winding road with other large, beautiful homes on it, Fran and I went to visit him there.

During the summer of 1984, the Olympics knocked many daytime shows on ABC off the air for much of the summer. Joe rented a house for Fran and me, and our almost one year old little girl, near his own weekend home. We loved the area and we decided to get a house there too some day. I would work on *Ryan's Hope* in the City during the week and come back to the house on the weekends. Lots of people upstate lived that way. Some went back and forth every day. Manhattan was just an hour and a half bus ride from New Paltz, and New Paltz was not very far from Stone Ridge, where Joe had his house.

During that summer of the Olympics I wrote a children's story about my daughter and the countryside around us. This was before the age of home computers with programs like "Word" that let you type and save and correct and revise and print and store so easily. So, it was written by hand on a long yellow legal pad.

I showed it to Joe. It was rough. Still, he liked it.

"A friend of mine is a publisher," Joe said. "We were roommates at Yale *many* years ago. I'll ask him if he'll take a look at this. I really like it."

Joe's "publisher friend" was a man named Richard Jackson who, along with a partner, created "Bradbury Press." I didn't know what "Bradbury Press" was and I had never heard of Richard Jackson. I couldn't Google him. There was no Google. I had no idea that Richard Jackson was the publisher of some of the most popular and loved children's books ever. He was the first to publish Judy Blume, Cynthia Rylant, Gary Paulsen, Avi, and many more authors.

I'm not sure if Joe gave Richard my hand-written story or if I brought him the story when I went to his office, but he did get it and he did read it and he did *not* like it.

"I can't just publish this because you are Joe's friend," he said. "I have a reputation as a publisher and this story isn't for me. I'm sorry. It just isn't strong enough."

Maybe because I didn't know the classic books he had published and all the awards his authors had won, I found the courage to say, "If I work on it some more, could I bring it back?" Or maybe I said that because publishing this story meant everything to me.

He sat there for a few seconds. He could have been

wondering if he should even bother to speak to me again. Or maybe he was already planning his lunch. But maybe he heard in my voice that writing wasn't just a whim of mine, and that I had been writing for most of my life.

"Okay," he said. "Work on it. And when you bring it back, for God's sake, have it typed. Nobody brings hand-written stories."

I revised. I re-wrote. I re-worked. Still by hand. As my 2-year-old daughter began to talk more and more, she helped me change the story from being a long, probably slow narra-tive, with no dialogue at all, into a shorter, brighter story that was *all* dialogue.

Meanwhile, my character on *Ryan's Hope*, Lazlo, was doing well. There were several permanent sets just for me: my apartment, my boxing gym, my favorite restaurant. These sets were saved so they could be hauled into place when I would be using them.

On my way home from the studio, I often got off the subway in Lower Manhattan and went to an old boxing gym to work out. I didn't actually box with anyone there. I would have been killed. But I worked out there and used the heavy bag and the speed bag and I watched what the real boxers did. It had been my idea to turn Lazlo into a boxer on the show, so I tried to learn the part. The boxing gym set on the show had speed bags and heavy bags and a boxing ring.

I got to know some of the boxers at the gym. One of them, a young man who was training for a Golden Gloves fight, had pretty much ignored me until one day he came to me and said, "Lazlo?"

I smiled and said, "Yeah. You watch *Ryan's Hope*?

"Yeah. Oh my God. Lazlo!" His name was Moses. He was really surprised, really happy to meet someone from "the stories." I was glad to get to know him and some of the other men at the gym.

When scenes on the show called for extras to be working out in the gym I invited Moses and Tyrone, another gym friend, to work with me. Tyrone was young, about twenty. He had been winning fights and getting close to going professional when he had to stop boxing completely. His eye was injured in a fight and the doctor told him he would lose that eye all together if he got hit again.

I went to see Moses fight at Madison Square Garden in the Golden Globe competition. The Garden was packed and I was up in the balcony, yelling my brains out when Moses was fighting. I was really glad when he won.

Every few months, while still on the show, I would call Richard Jackson and tell him I had a new version of the story I'd like him to see. He would invite me to his office and listen to me read the new version, and say something a little encouraging. And then say, "Keep working on it. I don't know what else to tell you." We did this for almost two years. Finally, I showed him my newest version and he said, "That's it. Let's just sharpen the ending now. And think of a title." When I came up with an ending that Richard and I liked, he said, "It's done. Let's decide on an illustrator."

Two years later, in 1988, *Rebecca's Nap*, my first book, was in book stores. It did well. Book stores had copies of *Rebecca's Nap* in their street-side windows. A major children's national book club chose *Rebecca's Nap* as the main selection. I had been living upstate for two years when the book came out, going to college evenings to become a teacher and working at a pre-school during the day.

A woman who came into the pre-school to pick up her son came over to the table I was working at and said, "Congratulations!"

"How come?" I asked her.

"I just got the new *Parents Magazine*"and your book is in it. It's a *Best Book of the Year*!"

16.5
Sendak

I took my two little girls to a Maurice
Sendak book
signing in Manhattan
where I stood in line and bought a paper-back
edition of
Where the Wild Things Are
and a *Max* doll, and Sendak signed both.
Two weeks later Joe and I went to the ballet
and then dinner,
then the limo driver took us back to Joe's apartment building on 5th Avenue and 11th Street.
Joe went inside to his apartment and I waited at
the street corner for a taxi.
A cab pulled up to the curb and a man got out
and held the door for me.
I said, "No thank you. I'm not getting in."
He said, "Looked like you were. Sorry."
I said, "I was, but I saw it was you.

You signed a 'Max' doll and a book for my kids
a little while ago.
I wanted to meet you."
He shut the cab door and said, "Okay.
What are you doing on 5ᵗʰ Avenue at 11:30
at night?"
"A friend of mine lives here.
We just got back from dinner.
I'm…I'm working on a book," I said.
"Oh? What kind of book?"
"A picture book. I've been working on it with
Richard Jackson
for a year now."
"I know Richard Jackson. Do you have time to
walk around the block," he said.
It was late and I still had to get back to Brooklyn
and then get up early
and go to the TV studio in Manhattan.
"Absolutely," I said.

I can't remember all that we talked about.
Probably about Joe and *Ryan's Hope*
and *Rebecca's Nap* and Fran and the kids.
By the time we circled back around
to 5th Avenue and 11th Street,
he said he'd like to see the book I was working on
and he would get in touch.
When we met again he read the latest draft of
<u>Rebecca's Nap</u>.
He said, "I was afraid it wouldn't be good.
Then what would I say?
But it's good."
Maurice never helped with my books or my
acting.
He never really helped with anything.
We were just friends.

17
Leaving Brooklyn

In 1986 Richard Jackson paid me an advance for *Rebecca's Nap*. That was the last thing he did before leaving Bradbury Press and moving to Orchard Books. He said it wasn't a big advance, but if the book went to a second printing, which it did, I would earn more. My *Ryan's Hope* adventure was coming to an end, and I could use the money. Fran and I talked it over and we figured if we spend the advance on rent and food it might last for a month or two in Brooklyn, or we could put the money toward getting a house up North and moving. I could drive to Manhattan from Ulster County if I had an audition.

Joe Hardy drove Fran and me upstate in February of 1986 during a snowstorm and the realtor in Stone Ridge took us to see some houses. One of them was a little house on almost 5 acres of land near Kerhonkson. The woman was selling it because she and her husband were getting back together after splitting up six months earlier, and she was moving up north to live with him.

We could see almost nothing outside the house because of the heavy snow and the inside was mostly a mess. Old worn-out wall-to-wall rugs on the floors, fat black plastic make-believe beams going across ceilings and wide, hollow, black plastic, make-believe molding lining the ceilings of most of the rooms. There was a lot of space out back that was hardly visible in the storm, so I asked the woman what the land was like in the summer.

"Oh, you know. Lots of green stuff. Plants and trees. And there is a brook that goes along the side of the house and into the woods in the back."

There was a really beat-up old dresser in the small dining room that was full of mouse crap. The owner told us, "You can keep this where it is or move it to the kitchen. Which ever you want." What!? I knew if all went well and we moved in, the shitty dresser would burn out in the back yard right away.

We signed some papers and the owner signed the papers and we gave the realtor a down payment (thank you Richard Jackson) and we went back to Brooklyn. There was something nice about the house, even with the plastic ceiling beams, old rugs, fake wood paneling and a landscape we couldn't see in the storm.

On Monday the realtor called and told us that five people had come in and wanted the house, some offering twenty thousand more than we were paying for it, but it was our house if we still wanted it because the owner had signed it over to us and we had put a down payment on it. We told him we would keep it.

We've been here almost forty years now and have no thoughts of leaving. I burned the mouse-hotel dresser the first day we moved in. I tore up the rugs and found beautiful old wide yellow-pine floors that we had experts sand and seal. I tore off all the plastic ceiling molding and I tore off the plastic paneling and I sheet-rocked, painted and cleaned. The brook was loud and fast in the spring and flowed into a wetland behind the house where shallow water flowed all year long from underground springs.

At first, I worked in a small restaurant in Stone Ridge. A job I hated. Just as I wasn't good at remembering lines when I was acting, I was even worse at remembering orders and who wanted them. On a busy night I was a maniac. There were only about ten tables in the whole place, with about four waiters taking orders, but I was still always a wreck.

The Hostess of the restaurant, the owner's sister, would come and tell each waiter when he or she had a new table. One crowded night she gave me a new table and then went about her business. I was serving dinners and drinks and taking orders and collecting money and I completely forgot about my new table.

About forty five minutes later, the Hostess came over and asked me if I took the order at the new table yet. I froze. My eyes opened wide. I swore inside my head. With as much disgust and loathing as she could find, she squeezed out through clenched teeth, "Never mind! I'll do it!" and turned and left.

I was an awful waiter.

I also worked with a builder during the day. Mostly outside. Sometimes doing roofs when it was fifteen below zero. Sometimes lying in wet, cold, crawlspaces putting insulation under the flooring.

For five dollars an hour.

After a couple years of this, and no new acting jobs and

fewer and fewer calls for auditions, I told Joe I was thinking about finishing college and becoming a teacher. I thought maybe he would find that idea kind of crazy and kind of late in life. I was almost forty and I had credit for only half a year of college, at the U of Alaska, Fairbanks, under my belt, from 1969.

But he thought it was a great idea. He hired me to take care of his home in Stone Ridge during the day so I could go to college at night in New Paltz. It took a while, but by 1991 I was substitute teaching and by 1993 I was hired as a 5th grade teacher at the local school.

17.5
Joe's House

I was inside Joe's house studying for a test
coming up at SUNY New Paltz where
I was learning to teach.
Barry, about Joe's age, (60?)
still came every week to mow the lawn,
even though I took care of the gardens.
Barry also worked at the community college
up the road as a grounds keeper.
. The phone rang. I picked it up and a woman
asked for Barry.
I went out on the deck and saw him
swirling around the yard on his riding mower.

I walked closer to him and waved my hands
and yelled as loud as I could, "Barry, telephone!"
He shut off his mower
and went inside and talked on the phone.
I stayed out on the deck to give him
some privacy.
When he came out a few minutes later
he stopped near me on his way back to the
mower and said,
"It's always some *fucking* thing.
My mother died."
A minute later he was riding the mower
around in circles again,
cutting the grass.

18
Getting Schooled

There I was again doing what I didn't do best: dealing with many people doing many different things all at the same time. Daily lesson plans for 5 or more daily subjects, report cards, going to night school to get my masters, staff meetings, and so many new people's names to remember. Somehow, I did it, and some kids would say I was their favorite teacher and some didn't like me. But after four years, the position of a literacy teacher for the 5th and 6th grades became available. And I really wanted it.

I was already working on getting a masters degree in literacy at New Paltz. My school principal took a long time to decide to let me have the position, but I celebrated when he did.

Sometimes I worked in other teachers' classrooms and sometimes I worked one-on-one with kids who needed some reading practice. I eventually had my own "Reading Room" where I set up a big turtle pond with a waterfall and a turtle sun-bathing rock. I got turtles from people who said things like, "I got my kid a turtle in kindergarten, and she's in college now. Do you want it?" I built a table and benches from wide pine slabs and small groups of kids, and I would read there or near the pond and write and talk. It usually went well. And the room was filled with books on shelves I had made all over the room.

I wrote lots of stories for my kids to read, based on their abilities and their interests. Lots of becoming a better reader happens by reading more, and at the right level, with some-one to help you when you need it. The kids liked the stories I wrote for them. They were the main characters. They also wrote their own stories, and a lot of them were fantastic. I still have them.

We turned books we read into plays, so the kids got to read their scripts over and over during rehearsals. We built settings, and made painting, drawing, and woodworking part of reading. We invited other classes and then put on the play. There was apple cider and doughnuts afterwards, for the actors and the audience.

I've kept the note below from a third grader I met when I was still a student teacher over thirty years ago. One of my projects with the class was to turn all of them into one long worm, each kid with his or her hands on the shoulders of the person in front. We went marching through the hallway and demonstrated the process of worm digestion. He wrote:

Dear Mr. Burstein

I liked the worm project. You are a good drawer. You will be a good teacher. I liked your books. When will you come again? My Birthday is in May. I was born in 1982 and that's when my dad left me.

18.5
Marriage at the Marriott

Fran and I and the kids were on our way back
to Kerhonkson
after visiting my brother Alan and my parents
in Connecticut.
I wasn't on TV anymore
and I was studying to become a teacher.
Driving through Fishkill, N.Y., our worn-out old
car died near the top of a one-way ramp
that swirled up from a Marriott Hotel.
I could let the car roll down to the hotel,
But I'd be going the wrong way.
No cars were driving up,
so we rolled down and parked.
We needed a pay phone.
We were supposed to be at Joe Hardy's house
later for dinner,
but now I had to cancel.
I had no idea how we would even get home.

We walked into the Marriott
and went right through a wedding
to get to the room with the phone booth.
Once inside, I called Joe.
He told me he cut his thumb.
"Slicing a *goddamn* onion!"
And I told him our "*goddamn* car broke down!"
— and we had no idea when or how
we would get home.
Then I called Larry, our neighbor in Kerhonkson.
He was a great helper and a fantastic mechanic.
"Larry, our car broke down in Fishkill.
It's dead!
Do you know anyone we could call
who would tow us back home?"
"Yeah," he said. "I do. Where are you?"
"We're at the Marriott."
"I'll be there in 45 minutes. Meet me in front."
"Wait. *You* don't have to…"
"Forty-five minutes. Meet me outside."
He hung up.
Larry didn't fool around.

When I pulled open the phone booth door
to leave,
the bride whose wedding
we had cut through stood
in front of me.
She was all fluffed up in her gown and long veil.
I was in my ripped old jacket
and my worn-out dungarees.
She said,
"It's my wedding day, Lazlo!
I can have anything I want.
And I want *you* *t*o kiss *me!*"
I stood up and tried not to touch her gown
with my muddy old jacket
and she leaned in, and we kissed.
She lifted her train off the floor
and went to finish getting married.
Fran, the kids, and I went outside
And waited, and waited, for Larry.

19
Last Call

I think I'll end with this memory of a dark day on an old subway car. I hadn't moved to Kerhonkson yet and I was still trying to get a new acting job in the City. I'd just been to an open call, which means you wait in line with lots of others until you see the casting director who has you read a page or two, will probably thank you for coming, and then get rid of you. I guess someone must have gotten a job after being seen on an open call, but I never knew anyone who did.

It was afternoon. I was headed for Brooklyn, and I was alone in a subway car. It was a very old train, covered in graffiti. The lights flickered for a while and then went dark and stayed dark. The empty, worn out seats and the dirty, un-swept floor added to the gloom of the ride. For a few seconds, when the subway passed a light on a tunnel wall, the darkness inside the car became more pronounced and the messes painted all over the windows and on the inside walls became more ugly. The train stopped, the doors opened, and about eight Middle-school boys got into the car.

They walked toward me and stopped close to my seat and stood there. Their skin was dark, the train was still dark, and the way they looked at me and then talked in a huddle seemed, to me, dark. It seemed like this was how it all would end. I wasn't afraid. No more auditions! There was nothing I could do. I thought, we are all going to die sometime. I'd fight as hard as I could to stay alive, to see my family again, but I knew the odds were against me.

Their huddle opened up and the students began rapping. The car was still dark, and I was still the only one in the car with the students. Their voices, their movements, their words, made the whole day brighten up. The threat of death had turned into an embrace. They had composed a song when they huddled together, and now they sang it. I don't remember all the words exactly. It went something like:

Riding where the train go
Sitting here is Laz-lo !
The king of the Stories
The man never worries
He kidnapped his bride
and took her for a ride!
Lazlo, Lazlo, he's Mr. Cool!
We're meetin' LAZLO
On the subway after school

Fred Burstein lives with his wife Fran in Kerhonkson, New York. They have two daughters who have their own homes now, and they have illustrated the four of Fred's books previously published by Irie Books. Fred is retired after having taught reading and writing in the local public school for over 20 years, a career he embraced after acting in Los Angeles and New York City. *My Life Acting, Writing, and Sometimes Boxing* is the ninth book of his that has been published.

Milton Keynes UK
Ingram Content Group UK Ltd.
UKHW022200131123
432512UK00002B/4